WOMENFOLKS

WOMENFOLKS
Growing Up Down South

Shirley Abbott

TICKNOR & FIELDS New Haven and New York 1983

Library of Congress Cataloging in Publication Data

Abbott, Shirley.
    Womenfolks, growing up down South.

    1. Women – Southern States.   2. Rural women –
Southern States.   3. Rural poor – Southern States.
4. Southern States – Social conditions.   I. Title.
HQ1438.A13A32   1983   305.4'0975   82-16880
ISBN 0-89919-156-8

Printed in the United States of America

S   10 9 8 7 6 5 4 3 2 1

For Katharine and Elizabeth
So that they can remember

Acknowledgments

Friends, family, and sometimes total strangers have been most willing to help me with this book. They have offered valuable criticisms, provided work space, and given other forms of essential encouragement. I particularly want to thank Cynthia and Charles Bonnes, Mary Cable, Paul F. Califano, Barbara Carlin, Sandra Cason, Priscilla Flood, Irwin Glusker, Barbara and Spencer Klaw, Zane and Norman Kotker, Charles L. Mee, Jr., Karen Meehan, James Parton, Margaret Pepperdene, Don Reed, Janet Reed, Lou Ann Sims, Chloe Steel, Alex Tomkievicz, and Donna Whiteman. To my aunts Frances Loyd, Emogene Loyd, and Laura Dyer I owe much, as to my uncles Russell Loyd and Cecil Loyd, and to my cousin Esther Allen; and, of course, to my mother, Velma, and my aunt Vera Wilson — two Loyd women no longer here. My cousin, more nearly my sister, June Owen not only shared her recollections but met planes, packed picnics, lent cars, and did anything else I asked of her. I am indebted as well to the New York Public Library, the Frederick Lewis Allen Room, and the Writers Room, where I completed much of my research.

Contents

WOMENFOLKS

One

Daughters of Time

We all grow up with the weight of history on us. Our ancestors dwell in the attics of our brains as they do in the spiraling chains of knowledge hidden in every cell of our bodies. These spirits form our lives, and they may reveal themselves in mere trivialities — a quirk of speech, a way of folding a shirt. From the earliest days of my life, I encountered the past at every turn, in every season. Like any properly brought up Southern girl, I used to spend a lot of time in graveyards.

On summer afternoons we'd pile into my mother's green Chevrolet — my aunt Vera, her daughter June (four years my senior), and often also some massive, aged female relation. Somehow we'd fit ourselves into the front and back seats, the women in print dresses and hairnets and no stockings, we two kids in shorts, and Mother would gun on down the road at 40 m.p.h. with every window open.

The boredom for my cousin June and me was as heavy as passion. Our mothers never packed a picnic basket or even a thermos of lemonade or any refreshments beyond a package of chewing gum, which they meted out late in the day half-a-stick at a time. June was not only older than I but smarter, and we'd soon be brawling. She knew the drill: she'd tease me about my freckles or who I "liked" ("It's that little drip Charles Lynas, ain't it?"), and like some perplexed, furious puppy, I'd attack. Since my aggression made the most racket, I got the punishment.

"Pinch a piece out of her, Vera," my mother would command — "peench" was how she said it — her hands tight on the wheel and her eyes on the dust boiling in the road. Vera would turn and apply the thumbscrew with pleasure and efficiency. I'd weep; June would giggle. The women were contemptuous of my sorrows, their object being to keep us silent so they could talk. What they talked about, mostly, was birthdays. They'd name over all the kin who had been born in September, marvel over how many of us had arrived in November (Billie Sue and Jessie, Laura Alice and Vel), try to puzzle out why so few came in May ("Nobody but just Olive on the fourteenth and Bonnie Sue on the fifth"). The heat of August must have been what depressed the May birthrate, but nobody reasoned it out that far, least of all me.

And on we'd go, down the road, sweating thigh to thigh and mopping our necks and suffering from thirst. Our agony was immaterial. The graves had to be visited, the weeds pulled off them, the markers read aloud, the flowers renewed. It was a shame to the living if the dead lacked flowers, an almighty disgrace if the next-of-kin had failed to buy a headstone.

In one sun-bleached old churchyard after another, the women would read the stones and recite the names and vital dates of those neglected souls who lacked markers. One or all of them would end up sobbing before we got back into the car. Somebody had to cry or else the afternoon would have been a waste. I always looked forward to the weeping. It broke the monotony. It was passionate and mystical. I loved it.

You cannot spend your summer afternoons in such pursuits without learning that the past matters. Southerners are famous for cherishing their fine old names, but we were not cherishing our fine old name. We were simply clinging to what had gone before, with our own fierce sense of propriety. Within our family there was no such thing as a person who did not matter. Second cousins thrice removed mattered. We knew — and thriftily made use of — everybody's middle name. We knew who was buried where. We all mattered, and the dead most of all.

That much, one way or another, was handed down. Little boys absorbed it, too, though the job of tomb guardians usually went to the women. It was by no means the only legacy. The past — not the one validated in schoolbooks but another kind, unanalyzed and undefined — hangs upon Southern women as if they were dispossessed royalty. To grow up female in the South is to inherit a set of directives that warp one for life, if they do not actually induce psychosis. This is true for high-born ladies as well as for farm women, and no one has ever quite explained it. A North Carolina journalist named Florence King made a good try, though, in a book called *Southern Ladies and Gentlemen.* All Southerners, she observed, are insane and most especially is the Southern woman insane. The reason is that "the cult of Southern womanhood endowed her with at least five totally different images and asked her to be good enough to adopt all of them. She is required to be frigid, passionate, sweet, bitchy, and scatterbrained — all at the same time. Her problems spring from the fact that she succeeds."

All this was true for me, too, except the bitchy part, for my mother was vigorously intolerant of bitchiness. But there are heavier elements in the mix besides. I grew up believing, though I could never have voiced it, that a woman might pose as garrulous and talky and silly and dotty, but at heart she was a steely, silent creature, with secrets no man could ever know, and she was always — always — stronger than any man. ("Now you don't have to let on about it," my mother would advise.) I never learned to construe the female sex as downtrodden or disadvantaged. I grew up under the hegemony of a line of magnificent women — strong women, with an ancient pedigree, who adhered to a code of honor, who oversaw my conduct, who held (and still hold) me responsible for my actions.

The South where I was born and raised was Arkansas, in a peaceable little resort town called Hot Springs. When I was a child, just before World War II began, there were two main local industries: the legal one was applying healing waters to the sick and the illegal one was gambling. The yearly race meet — which was not only legal but operated by the sovereign state of Arkansas — also caused some cash to flow in a favorable direction, if only on a seasonal basis.

People sometimes ask me whether a town like Hot Springs in the middle of a state on the wrong side of the Mississippi can really have been the South. Yes, it was, for sure. Arkansas was short on mint juleps and azalea gardens and had nothing to compare with the charms of Natchez, but it was plenty Southern. Contrary to what they showed in the movies in those days, the South didn't mean bourbon and hoop skirts, it meant red dirt and poor people, which we had in abundance. We also had our share of Southern historical monuments. Not antebellum mansions or statues of Robert E. Lee on his horse, for you could drive from Fayetteville to El Dorado and then backtrack to Texarkana without ever seeing any such thing. What you would see were shanties, tar-paper houses, tumbledown barns, and chickens scratching industriously for bugs in totally bald front yards. In those days if a car passed yours on the road, you'd have to roll the windows up or even pull over in the ditch and wait until the dust storm died down.

When President Roosevelt made his radio talk about one third of the nation being ill fed, ill clothed, and ill housed, I wasn't yet born, but as I was to learn, the third he had in mind lived chiefly below the Mason-Dixon line. With or without magnolias, the South stretched from the Atlantic coast into the foothills of Georgia, the Carolinas, Virginia, and Kentucky, down the skinny backbone of the Appalachians, on across the Mississippi into Oklahoma and east Texas. In that down-on-its-luck landscape, nothing had changed much since the Civil War. It was farmland or wasteland. Within it little towns and cities eked out their livings like respectable elderly ladies taking in sewing. In Hot Springs the needlework was a little fancier than in, say, Tuscaloosa, Alabama, but the South was where I lived, all the same.

When Roosevelt called us a national problem, it didn't particularly hurt anybody's feelings that I can recall. We were glad he cared, and we were used to having a depression. Other folks had steel mills and assembly lines. We had our own ways of getting along. We had, for example, our rootedness to one spot, which, since massive numbers of Southerners were already migrating west and north, was a state of mind rather than a fact. We had our odd speech patterns, which came from our ancestors rather than our schoolteachers. We had our mistrust of progress, a *modus vivendi* of which we were utterly ignorant. And we had our resignation or discouragement or contentment — whichever you wanted to call it.

All this, of course, ran cross-grained to go-getting Americanism. Even through World War II, with the voice of the President to energize us, we felt more like Southerners than Americans. I used to search the sky hopefully for Messerschmidts, but in my heart I knew they'd be divebombing real places like Schenectady and Pittsburgh and Dayton. We didn't even have a civil defense program, just rationing — but we'd always had rationing, one way or another. Nevertheless we were proud to be Southerners. Nobody knew why.

This curious sense of separateness is one of the most stubbornly preserved Southern attitudes. The South, its historians say, stands apart from other American regions because of its peculiar history. History has been cruel to Southerners, has persistently dealt them deuces. The bloodiest war ever fought in this hemisphere was fought in the meadows and mountains and cities of the South. It killed and ravaged us, and to my grandparents, when I was little, it still seemed like yesterday. The most eloquent of Southern historians, C. Vann Woodward, has put the matter plainly: "Southern history, unlike American, includes large components of frustration, failure, and defeat. It includes not only an overwhelming military defeat but long decades of defeat in the provinces of economic, social, and political life."

All Southerners have at some moment tasted the bitterness of their own history, if only in the images of rubes and nitwits that pass for Southerners in film and television. And they have tasted its sweetness, too, as have outsiders, if only in the unwonted courtliness that can manifest itself in a roadside diner or any other unlikely spot. History isn't something fancy to most Southerners. It's painful, pleasurable, and concrete. It's whatever Mother and Aunt Vera and June and I were seeking in those graveyards.

My mother and the other women I knew as a child were farm women, one or two generations removed from the real pioneer days, gentled and domesticated by the time I came among them. But the marks were there. Their skins were leathery from working outdoors. Some of these women were serene, and some, hot-tempered, and in either case they brooked no transgressions of their notions of morality, and woe to the mortal who spoke to these women with disrespect. They were not innocent or submissive or delicately constituted, not afraid of balky cows or chicken hawks. It took them approximately two hours to transform a live rooster into Sunday dinner. They could reason with a mule and shoot a gun. But they also knew just how to take hold of a baby and what to say to a weeping two-year-old.

I used to hang on the backs of their chairs as they peeled peaches by the bushel and talked about how to keep dill pickle jars from exploding, and why Cousin Rosity had got the cancer she was dying from, and what effect the drought would have on cattle prices, and how the doctors had decided to cut off poor old Uncle Jules' leg ("Orght to be ashamed of themselves, him being ninety and about dead anyhow of that diabetes"), but danged if the old man hadn't got up off his bed and run them out of his house. Sometimes, thinking the children out of earshot, or perhaps deeming us old enough to hear, they would forget their ironclad morals and recount some scandal that was simmering in a cottage down the road a piece or even tell a bawdy joke. Never anything explicit, merely the gropings of newlyweds, forever doomed to get the Vaseline mixed up with the glue. In later years, when I was adolescent, it shocked me to hear them laugh out loud about such things. How could they joke about anything so awesome? Had they no sense of romance?

Then when the peaches were peeled and sliced into half a dozen enamel dishpans, they would make me stand at a tub of scalding, soapy water and wash out Kerr-Mason jars by the case. It took a child's hand for that. Theirs were too splayed. I have watched those knobby brown fingers laying French plaits into my cousin June's black hair, my own being too fuzzy to braid, and I have known those women to walk five miles to spend an afternoon at a quilting frame. It never occurred to me then that they were carriers and conservators of a culture of their own, one that I would have to unravel one day and reknit.

Other Southern women were part of my life too, infinitely more primitive than my own relatives, with roots even further back in time. Until I was thirteen my father had earned a living mainly as a gambler — a bookmaker, I mean, in one of the illegal Hot Springs horsebooks. Then an agrarian fit momentarily took hold of him, and he moved us to a forty-acre farm west of Hot Springs. But what we had was barren ground. The apple orchard that he planted in high hope never bore. The well constantly threatened to go dry. We scarcely dared flush the toilet or bathe. Urban spirit that I was, I had no more aptitude as a farmer's daughter than my father had as a farmer. I hated digging potatoes, and I hated gathering eggs. I hated the smell of chicken houses — vinegary, sweet, rotten — despised the chickens, shrank from the finger-skinning work that went on seven days a week, indoors and out. As I loaded the wire egg baskets, hoping not to infuriate the ill-humored old hens, I comforted myself with the thought that I had, after all, not been born for such indignities.

But there was an escape. On summer afternoons I would go across the road and sit with Grandma Lizzie Ethridge (not my grandma, of course, but the county's). It was a voyage back through the centuries. We'd sit under a shade tree together, and she would try to teach me to crochet. ("Make them little picots nice and even," she would command, although she called them "peekholes.") I would stay and stay, laboriously chaining around my doily. At five o'clock when I should have crossed the road again to help my parents with the chores, I would follow her on her rounds instead.

Lizzie Ethridge was scarcely five feet tall, and from planting time to harvest she never put on a shoe. Though she kept herself very clean, she always smelled faintly of sweat. She wore a sunbonnet when she walked outside, and a print housedress with a one-piece overall apron. At the neck of her dress, the trimming on her homemade "princess slip" showed. This was a loose cotton garment that she never went without, even in the hottest weather. Under these various modest layers were the mighty contours of a paleolithic stone goddess — the Venus of Willendorf — with vast breasts spreading atop a bulging belly. I would follow Granny down her rows of corn and pole beans or among her flower beds, watching as she bent over each blossom with a bucket of water and a dipper. The flowers would have made a botanist gape. They were profuse, exotic, tropical. She sent off for seeds advertised on the radio and, having no idea of the names of things, made up her own classes and genuses.

When we sat down to rest, she would tell stories, pausing now and then to pack her lower lip with snuff or spit the sickly brown liquid into a tin can. She had come into this county as a child some eighty years before, "from way over yonder," she said, waving a finger toward the eastern hills. She had helped clear a homeplace and plant a crop. She had heard mountain lions scream at night, had watched a milk snake drink from a cow's udder in the light of dawn, had been saved by the Lord Jesus, and baptized in a running stream. Had ridden home alone bareback one night from a brush-arbor tabernacle, the horse at full gallop and a panther running behind. She had married young and borne many children, some of whom died in infancy, some of whom, now old themselves, looked in on her from time to time.

Every day she made her way through a portion of the Scriptures. She knew the chapter and verse in Deuteronomy that calls it an abomination against God for women to wear men's clothing. She spoke of the beast that would rise up — in our own lifetime — out of the sea, with seven heads and ten horns and upon his horns ten crowns and upon his heads the name of blasphemy, and by what other signs and portents we would recognize that the Second Coming was at hand. She would tell me that God was on the side of America and the nation of Israel. And while she pieced the news of the world and the Book of Revelations together into a crazy quilt, she would take a spool of thread and a tatting shuttle no longer than her fingers and knot a length of lace as fine as any I had ever seen.

Even then she was an anachronism, one of the last inhabitants of a mountain peak on a slowly sinking continent. She carried her ignorance with her, and her wisdom, as well. My own family had drawn close to the modern world, if not become part of it, but Granny Ethridge never had. Yet she was a Southern woman as much as any Scarlett O'Hara, and she became one of the ancestors in my mind's attic, my connection with the seventeenth century — perhaps the seventeenth century B.C.

I know perhaps a dozen people still living who possess the ancient attitudes arising from their solid, tangible connections with this neolithic past. Every year the number of them diminishes. Every year one homeplace or another gets torn down. Even when I was a child, the Southern past, palpable as it was, was hard to unearth in any articulated form. Like most children, I perceived my own family past as a mystery understood, I supposed, by my parents and manifested — if I could perceive it — in my surroundings. To find the potsherds and the clues took an archaeologist's eye, even in those days. Like all small towns, Hot Springs, where I spent my childhood, looks simple but is not. Compared with New Orleans, it is an insignificant western upstart. Hardly anything was there — except hot water — before 1870. And yet it is older than the dinosaurs.

The town sits in a vale between two rounded-off, thickly wooded mountains. Hot mineral waters pour out of the mountainsides, and the hills for miles around erupt with springs, some of them famous and commercial, with bottled water for sale, others trickling under rotten leaves in deep woods and known only to the natives. From one spring the water gushes milky and sulphurous. From another it comes forth laced with arsenic. Here it will be heavy with the taste of rocky earth, there, as sweet as rainwater. Each spring possesses its magical healing properties and its devoted, believing imbibers. In 1541, on the journey that proved to be his last, Hernando de Soto encountered friendly tribes at these springs. For a thousand years before him the mound-building Indians who lived in the Mississippi Valley had come here to cure their rheumatism and activate their sluggish bowels.

The main street of town, cutting from northeast to southwest, is schizoid, lined on one side with plate-glass store fronts and on the other with splendid white stucco bathhouses, each with its noble portico and veranda, strung along the street like stones in an old-fashioned necklace. All but one of the bathhouses are closed down now. At the head of the street, on a plateau, stands the multistoried Arlington, a 1920s resort hotel and a veritable ducal palace in yellow sandstone. Opposite, fronted in mirrors and glittering chrome, is what once was a gambling casino and is now a wax museum. "The Southern Club," it was called in the days when the dice tumbled across the green baize and my father waited for the results from Saratoga to come in over Western Union. Lots of other horsebooks operated in that same neighborhood — the White Front, the Kentucky Club — some in back rooms and dives in which no respectable person would be seen. But the Southern was another thing. Gamblers from Chicago strolled in and out in their ice-cream suits and their two-tone shoes and nothing smaller than a C-note in their pockets. Packards pulled up to the door and let out wealthy men with showy canes and women in silk suits and alligator pumps who owned stables of thoroughbreds and next month would travel to Churchill Downs. I saw this alien world in glimpses as Mother and I sat at the curb in the green Chevrolet, waiting for the last race at Belmont or Hialeah to be over so that my father could figure the payoffs and come home to supper.

The other realm was the usual realm, Middletown, Everyplace. Then it was frame houses, none very new. Now it is brick ranches and splits, carports, inlaid nylon carpet, and draw-drapes. Now the roads are lined with a pre-fab forest of Pizza Huts, Bonanzas, ninety kinds of hamburger stand, and gas stations, some with an occasional Southern touch: a plaque, for example, that reads "Serve-U-Sef." In what I still remember as horse pasture now stands a windowless high school — windowless — where classes range up to one hundred, and the teacher may not be able to learn everybody's name. My old elementary school, a two-story brick thing that threatened to fall down, had windows that reached to the fourteen-foot ceiling. We kept them shut only from November to February, for in this pleasant land the willows turn green and the winds begin sweetening in March, and by April the iris and jonquils bloom so thickly in every yard that you can smell them on the schoolroom air. On an April afternoon, we listened to the creek rushing through the schoolyard and thought mostly about crawdads.

At first the town had been only a country village, which is almost obliterated now but visible still in the feed store, the occasional market that sells local produce rather than tomatoes trucked in from California, the one surviving dry-goods store where a flesh-and-blood saleslady will patiently hunt up your size in long-handled cotton underwear, the cavernous brown courthouse with its marble floors and nonfunctioning ceiling fans, and in sagging old frame houses on quiet outskirts streets. These are the vestiges of an unfinished, unpolished place that served first as a marketplace and supply depot for the farmers, and then was the place they came, in hope or defeat, when they abandoned their farms and moved to town to rent a house and look for work.

Out there in the sticks, miles east and north of Hot Springs, is where my matrilineal origins lie: the burial grounds are there. My mother was, by any definition, an authentic Southerner. Her ancestors had lived on the stony hillsides of Arkansas, Mississippi, Tennessee, Alabama, Georgia, and the Carolinas for as far back as anybody could remember, having migrated across the South generation by generation — from a rock to a hard place. That is a catch phrase now, tossed around by guys in ad agencies, but as invented in the Southern backwoods, it was pure poetry. Like most Southern farmers, and indeed the vast majority of white Southerners, Mother's ancestors never owned slaves, and when they took up arms for the Confederacy, did it unwillingly. They were backwoodsmen, not warriors. If they got anything out of the Civil War, it was quadruple reinforcement of their conviction that hard times were permanent and would probably get worse, and that you'd better be tough enough to look after your own.

Mother never had much to say about all this. Henry Ford thought history was bunk, and Mother did, too. Nevertheless, she was shackled by it and carried it with her in those ancestral attitudes of independence, as well as in the knowledge of how to quilt and sew, put up preserves, and generally make out with what you had. It was a useful lesson to draw from the ages, and she drew it.

From my father, definitely not an authentic Southerner, I learned something different about the light of history — for he valued the past, too, but not the way Mother did. As a growing girl I had to absorb his past, and in no way did his resemble Mother's. He hated clannishness and family reunions as much as he hated fried okra and turnip greens, and he wouldn't set foot in a cemetery unless the funeral of his next-of-kin was actively under way. Of his family history he refused to speak. Somewhere in his mysterious youth he had learned to lay odds and figure bets. He was a one-man parimutuel machine, could tell you the payoff on a three-horse parley without ever putting pencil to paper, and he never made a mistake. Lawbreaker that he was, he set off every morning in a fedora and a three-piece suit and tie, just like everybody else's daddy. He might well have been working for the electric company, except that the governor never sent the state police to raid the electric company, whereas occasionally my father had to post bail. He liked to describe himself as a cum laude graduate of the school of hard knocks, and for sure he had got knocked about, but he lacked all street cunning. All his ideas came from books. And most of his ideas were about history, which was definitely not bunk to him: it was the fountain where you saved your soul.

Unlike the men in Mother's family, who were as taciturn as Vermonters, my father had the "gift of gab," as he loved calling it, and since I was an only child, often sick, or bored or in need of a playmate, I was a ready audience for tales. So he soon plugged me in to his version of the history of the Old South, with excursions into Antiquity.

We lived on an unpaved Hot Springs street, in a modest white frame house of Victorian vintage, with an ample slope of lawn, plenty of pine trees and wild cherries, hedges of snowball bushes, a redbud tree and a flowering peach by the side of the house, trellises of roses all around the porch, and hidden in this bower, a porch swing. I often sat there with my father on Sundays, or stood at his heels in the afternoons as he knelt with his trowel and weeded the flower beds. And in this scene of placidity and peace, he would summon up those regiments of gray warriors flourishing their sabers, those cavalry horses pounding their proud hooves, Stonewall Jackson standing in a hail of Minié balls and buckshot and God only knew what else, John Bell Hood strapping himself to his saddle after his leg was shot off, Jeb Stuart capturing a whole Yankee cavalry regiment and sending Lincoln a wire about the poor quality of the horse-flesh: Oh God, those splendid, besashed, befeathered, bare-footed heroes in a doomed cause! And in command of them, Lee, the man of sorrows, whom I used to confuse with Jesus Christ.

I heard about those long gray lines at Gettysburg, and how the damyankees couldn't believe that men could be so brave, and the dauntless women at home battling all alone (with the aid of the customary loyal darkies) to save the Big House, the vast, savage battle at Shiloh where so many thousands fell that the streams ran red with blood for months after. Then Daddy would work up to the set piece: Reconstruction, the unspeakable vengeance devised by the angry victors who reserved for the South the same fiery portion that the Greeks had visited on Troy and who sowed our fields with salt as the Romans had done at Carthage. God, I loved that part, and he did, too, and it made no difference to him or to me that he had been born and raised in Goshen, Indiana, and that his forefathers had gone to war in blue coats.

My father would have acknowledged with cheers C. Vann Woodward's brilliant insight into Southern history — that it is woven of failure, defeat, and disappointment, and that "such a heritage affords the Southern people no basis for the delusion that there is nothing whatever beyond their power to accomplish." The history of the South that mattered most to him was pure hallucination, but it won't go away, no matter how many times it is debunked. It consists — this is a quick survey — of slim aristocratic planters, all descendants of the Duke of Monmouth, each with rolling tracts of land, each an enlightened architect of an agrarian civilization snuffed out, alas, in 1865 or thereabouts. It consists of the notion that Reconstruction was a

disastrous miscarriage of justice. It consists of the malignant notion that black people are, on the one hand, too
savage and on the other too childlike to survive as a free
people. It consists of the equally malignant notion that
segregation was the bedrock of the Southern way of life.

This home-grown aristocracy compares favorably of
course with the English gentry from which every Southern
aristocrat believes he descends. One of the few unfailingly
popular commodities that the South has exported is its
perennial operetta with the Southern gentleman and his
charming lady and his faithful retainers and his vast plantation. Next door to him dwells a Jeffersonian yeoman. Farther off in the hills swarms a race of verminous hillbillies
and assorted white trash, making whiskey and children. It
is as orderly as the scenes of peace in some late-medieval
book of hours, where the peasants till the green fields under
a sapphire sky, and the lord rules in his gilt-turreted cas-
tle — a made-to-measure cosmos that provides a comfortable contrast with the root-hog-or-die ethic of Yankeedom,
which took hold of the country irrevocably when the gates
of Eden swung shut after the Civil War.

My father, of course, earnestly believed in all this. How
could he not? It was made for him. He was at heart a
homeless man, with no real profession, and until he settled
tentatively down in Arkansas, no sense that he might belong in one place. He was the eldest son of a turn-of-the-
century Gothic pair from Indiana — a father given to public rectitude and private rages, a mother always terrified
and ill, who had taken permanently to her bed after the
birth of her second child. Abandoned by this tormented
menage at the age of ten and then peremptorily reclaimed
by them a year later, he in his turn had fled at the age of
sixteen on the top of a fast freight. He meant to go to San
Francisco and join the merchant marine, but after many
overland voyages and one broken marriage and an un-
countable number of jobs (steel-mill hand, vacuum-cleaner
salesman, floorwalker, candy maker, and bootlegger were

the ones he admitted to), he ended up in Arkansas where he married my mother and settled down to become a Southerner.

He grasped the usefulness of Southern history instantly. The Greeks and the Romans were almost as handy. He would read aloud to me from various English historians or retell Thermopylae or the Fall of Carthage in his own versions. But whether at Actium or Chancellorsville, he always took the proceedings personally and carefully positioned his sympathies in the losing camp. He was for Hector against the Greeks, Athens against Sparta, Hannibal against the Romans, Vercingetorix against Julius Caesar, and Marc Anthony against Augustus, but he rooted for Imperial Rome against the Goths. Edward Gibbon's *Decline and Fall of the Roman Empire* was the book he loved. How he savored the melancholy theme, the perfectly wrought neoclassical prose! He used to read the more dramatic passages aloud to me, and the arrival of the Visigothic chief, Alaric, at the gates of Rome was a favorite selection.

"The first emotions of the nobles and of the people were those of surprise and indignation, that a vile barbarian should dare to insult the capital of the world," he would intone — he stretched on the sofa in his sock feet, and I in the deep cushions of an upholstered rocker — and then continue, "That unfortunate city gradually experienced the distress of scarcity, and at length the horrid calamities of famine," and so on through Gibbonian descriptions of feeding on carcasses — "mothers are said to have tasted the flesh of their slaughtered infants!" — and of the stench of the unburied thousands who had expired from hunger in the streets of Rome.

I must have been the only child in Hot Springs who had nightmares about the Visigoths, and I could not share any of what my father taught me with my peers. They would have thought I was crazy. History to them was the acres of fine print in the fifth-grade textbook. How could I have explained to them what satisfaction it is to wallow perpetually in mythology, to see all human life as a confrontation between the good guys and the bad guys, an unending Saturday afternoon serial. And romance came into it as well. Scarcely had I learned "Horatius at the Bridge" by heart before my father introduced me to *Gone With the Wind*, which I read more times than a Baptist preacher reads the Ten Commandments and with the same flinty faith. Better to walk with righteous Southerners, I told myself, than Yankee devils. Let 'em burn Twelve Oaks. We won't give in.

And so with the guidance of my Yankee father, I grew to womanhood listening to the footfalls of Robert E. Lee, Pierre Gustav Toutant Beauregard, and a number of equally noble Greeks and Romans. Wherever in the history books my father could find some runestone that deciphered into "you have beaten me, but I'm better than you are anyhow," he seized on it and gave it an accession number in the underdogs' museum. Homeless he may have been to the end of his days, a lover of the long shot that steps high and runs out of the money, but he found nourishment and dignity in the South and in the chronicle of defeat. Whatever the nature of the Southern identity, my father isolated one element of it and made himself Southern by absorbing it. He never voiced it, but something like this went through his head: "I'm not like you, and though you may send an army against me, I won't give up, and I won't change my ways either, and the reason I won't is that I'm better than you."

This, of course, is the voice of the whipped and defiant, the underground. Blacks have said the same of themselves against whites. It is no accident that the idea of passive resistance occurred to Martin Luther King, Jr. when and where it did, though he attributed the notion to Gandhi. Men of all races, indeed, have used the tactic against all manner of terrifying antagonists — the church, the law, the military. And women have used it against men. If Southern history has no other meaning, this is the one worth preserving: that there is something better than success, than being top dog, than having the habit of command.

So this was the lesson I learned over the years, trying to

piece my father's version of the past together with my mother's. Later, as an adult, I learned that in Southern history are thickets and swamps of ill-perceived, half-forgotten myths, and many kinds of women. Some of them are now emerging in the hands of a new school of academic historians who know where to look for them: mistresses of plantations who knew as much about plantations as their lords and masters, and worked as hard as any slave. Black women struggling against all odds to hang on to their beliefs, their sanity, and their families — not victims but heroines. Tenant farmers' wives in the 1930s bearing and raising a dozen children and doing the work of a man besides and never complaining or dropping dead in their tracks. Such women as these existed, and they were not Southern ladies and belles. They bear witness to something buried, unvoiced, powerful.

And so I began to think about my maternal ancestors as representatives of a Southern feminine culture worth remembering. They were independent almost from birth. They knew how to make do in harsh circumstances, and even in clement surroundings they maintained a stubborn equilibrium with their menfolks. To a degree that infuriated me and eventually drove me away from them, they gritted their teeth and were selfless, made sacrifices, and gave in. I am not like them. Yet I am of them, mindful of their legacy wherever I go.

Two

Good Country People

Like many another primitive society, the rural South has been all but swept off the edge of the earth in the twentieth century. The very essence of a primitive culture, of course, is that it keeps few records of its thoughts and ways, and its relics are never put into museums until they have become just that: relics. If anything of the backwoods South can be preserved, it will be through that peculiar kind of history that transmits itself by other means — in the features of a face, in gesture, a turn of phrase, or what a family chooses to remember about itself.

I was born into this culture very late and only half way, and my corner of it consists now of a dwindling number of elderly relations, a few old family connections, and one place where I still can go and stand on my home ground. That is a house way out in Garland County, Arkansas, north of Hot Springs, where my Aunt Frances and Uncle Cecil live. Farmers and frontier people by inheritance, they have struggled all their lives to stay on the land, sometimes risking starvation in the process. It has been twenty years since they tried seriously to farm; both of them have had to work for wages.

But they still live, if not in the same house, at least in the same county where they have always lived, near a sawmill town called Mountain Pine. (It is the property of Weyerhauser, "the Tree Company," which the locals do not regard as a benefactor of the laboring classes.) The sawmill, under various owners, has been there as long as I can remember, a kind of topside coal mine — noisy, dangerous work with an inexorable tendency to destroy the worker. I remember Frances's grief when Cecil first had to sign on there; now two of their grandsons work at the mill. It is only a few miles from the place where some hundred-odd years ago Cecil's forebears and mine cleared a space in the wilderness and founded a little village, now long gone.

The drive to their house is long, first on a two-lane hardtop, then down two progressively narrowing dirt roads. Either the dust or the mud, depending on the season, is sure to take the shine off the car, and some of the family used to use that as a reason for not going out there. Cecil and Frances live alone now, having raised five children and one grandchild, all of them out and married. Their house is painted green and has a kind of shored-up look with the front porch braced on two-by-fours and no handrails for the concrete steps. It was a three-room shack when Cecil made the down payment on it some thirty years ago. Plank by plank he turned it into a house: now they even have a bathroom. In the front room are two vinyl easy chairs, one of which, as you come through the screen door, is likely to be filled with Aunt Frances. Cecil's favorite chair is a highbacked wooden rocker. There is a vinyl-covered divanette, as we call it, where I always settle down. The most massive piece in the room is a high steel hospital bed, made up with an immaculate white sheet. It serves as a daybed, and Cecil sleeps here sometimes. He has been at the mercy of the heart surgeons lately.

The floor is linoleum, green like the window shades. The curtains droop with age. On the wall is a large framed picture of Jesus the Good Shepherd, and all around are photographs of the grandchildren and grandnephews and grandnieces. In winter the woodbox is full of kindling, and the iron stove heats this small parlor to 85 degrees, while in the two back bedrooms your teeth chatter. The largest room is the kitchen. Frances now has a gas range, an electric refrigerator, and hot running water, but I have eaten many a meal there and then washed dishes in well water that had been heated on the stove.

Whenever I come, all my cousins and their husbands and wives and children gather (partly out of deference to my mother, I am sure, who is dead now but was greatly loved in this house). My daughters, aged three and seven, cling to my legs, for there is much kissing and clasping and laughing, and they hope to escape whatever whiskery embraces they can. I used to be just one of the numberless band of cousins here, but I am a Northerner now, an apartment dweller whose children ride subways and think Riverside Park is the great outdoors. "Lord," I hear a small boy observe of my elder child, "don't she talk funny?"

While we ask all the usual questions about health and weather and absent relatives, learning something but not much from the answers, my aunt puts a Southern dinner on the table: pork chops and cream gravy, a platter of fried chicken, a vast square pan of dressing with the giblets in it, green beans simmered all day with onions and a piece of salt meat, a dish of fried okra, which I especially love, sliced tomatoes so solid and delectable as to suffice for dinner all by themselves, homemade relishes and pickles, white beans and ham hock, field peas cooked for an eternity and served with hot peppers on the side, fresh biscuits and cornbread — fine-textured, sour, flat, white cornbread made from stone-ground meal and buttermilk. There are a few things missing: the brick of fresh-churned butter, the bowl of clabber, the pitcher of warm buttermilk with the yellow flecks still swimming in it — they don't keep a cow these days.

We eat this feast in shifts around an enormous oak table

set with ten plates at a time. Frances, who refuses to sit down until everyone else has eaten, moves around the kitchen, refilling our iced tea glasses or ladling up saucerfuls of deep-dish fruit pies and blackberry cobbler. No self-respecting mountain woman would sit while the men are eating — and this is by no means a gesture of womanly humility. With the small children she is endlessly tender, leaning over them to ask if they like their milk and instantly supplying them with tea or soda pop if they don't, buttering their biscuits and spooning up honey, admonishing their mothers not to fuss at them for eating too much pie and no vegetables. This is a granny's license: when Frances was a young mother, she made the kids behave. Babies, though, she always petted and adored.

As I watch her go from stove to table to sink, I recall what she once told me about her childhood, which she spent in an orphanage, until at the age of ten she was adopted by a farm family in this county and turned into a washerwoman and cook. In order that her stepsister might attend school on washdays, Frances stood over the rub-board. When she was eighteen, Cecil rescued her from this indenture. It was hardly Cinderella and Prince Charming, but the hardship he offered her was at least their own. The overalls on the rub-board now belonged to him. After such a childhood she ought to have been permanently angry, but she took readily to the idea of love. Of course she and Cecil frown and grumble a great deal at one another, but what holds them together goes beyond mere love.

Cecil is as linear as a hickory tree in winter and unbent. His black hair is white now, but as thick and wiry as ever, and the swarthy Indian skin, which was always stretched too tightly over the sharp bones of his face and leathery from the sun and wind, even when he was young, is now disfigured with random albino blotches, for which the doctor offers no explanations. Cecil is thin-lipped and blue-eyed and grave, like a hillbilly, but his grin has a wild, unbeaten quality. He smiles often at me. We love each other unabashedly, for in my countenance he sees his little sister, and in his I see something I can hardly name, a bobcat that comes out of the Southern mountains and will not be whipped.

I fill my plate twice over, and Cecil tells me I'll fade away if I can't do better than that. "You're pore as a snake," he says, "skinny as a fence railing," though indeed I am not. We all stuff ourselves, and then after the usual protestations, eat a big helping of pie. It is a ritual banquet, of course, almost as exceptional to them as to me. For half of what is on the table has come from the supermarket, not the garden or the smokehouse or the cellar. No one, least of all Arkansas farm families, eats like this any more. There aren't hands enough at home to do the cooking or mouths to do the eating, and prices are too high. Cecil could have made do with green beans and Wonder bread, and the pleasures of the country table are forbidden to Frances, who has ulcers and is supposed to be losing fifty pounds.

After lunch, while the women wash dishes, Cecil takes my daughters and helps them catch the eight cats who live under the front porch. All the cats have names. Then he and the girls go down to the barn, and he gives them a ride on the mule (which stands squint-eyed, foreleg bent, at the gate), and takes them to the pigsty where a hog named Harold fattens, and to the dog run where three hounds wag and yap. The best squirrel dogs in the county, Cecil says. He is a connoisseur of dogs, for he has always been a hunter, and there were years when the game he shot was food for the family. "Cecil thinks more of them dogs than he does me," is one of Frances's favorite remarks, and Cecil always agrees. "I could sell my dogs for six hundred dollars, and I couldn't get nothing for you." My elder daughter eyes them solemnly. "Did Uncle Cecil mean that?" she inquires later. "Oh, no, darling," I say. Frances, overhearing us, laughs.

They are my last connection with a way of life that formed my mother, and her mother, all my maternal ancestry and therefore, in ways I hope I can discover, me. The traditions go back to the Picts and the Celts, no doubt, back to hardships that broke the back and the heart, but bred strong and insubordinate women. I sit here at my aunt's table, wondering why it did. As I survey these faces, especially those of my women cousins, who are inheritors of the tradition in surer ways than I, I see that strength in them, and I wonder if I, too, have the gene. June and Linda, Frankie Lou and Donna and Annette (my name in this place is still Shirley Jean) — we sit around the oak table, now gleaming clean, with the platters of leftovers cooling off at the center under a dish towel. We are not like our mothers. The old commonality is gone.

Some of us have come here from far away. One is rich, one very poor, one has a graduate degree, one lacks a high school diploma. One is twice divorced, two wish they were divorced, none has borne more than three children. But we try to bond together and to talk in the old way, of kids and doctor bills and cookpots and the price of groceries. Linda tells us about the new preacher and how he saved twenty souls at revival last month. I have never heard him preach and never will. She recalls the days when her twin sons were a year old, and there was a new baby besides — we were all somewhere else at the time. We wonder about Aunt Olive, off in California and just having had a breast removed. They tell me about Miss Lessie Trammel's funeral, which I missed. The stories are mundane, but the steadfastness of these women is not. If they were in a corporate board room, they could hardly display more intelligence and control.

The legacies from another world that exist in Cecil's house and yard may not last long enough for my daughters to remember them, except as a faint recollection of the broad back of a mule and the coprolitic stink of a pigsty and an aunty who told them they needn't drink their milk, never mind what Mama says. Can I transpose them into that other dimension where remembrances live that are not even mine but my mother's, her mother's? This great-uncle of theirs who looks like an aging Indian chieftain was their grandmother's big brother. When she was six, he took her out in a rowboat, threw her in the water, and told her to swim.

She swam. When she was eight, he took her to the fields and taught her how to shoot a .22. When she was ten he cut down cedar trees and planed the wood and carved the large fine chest that now sits in my bedroom in New York filled with the quilts she made. Every summer they picked cotton together, partners on the long rows, Grandpa's flying aces, sweating in the blazing sun and hating the prickles that made their fingers raw, but poking rude fun at their younger brother who would sit down with his tow-sack at the end of his row and weep.

Together they knew the great-grandmother of my children, who to me is only a shadow, a face in a picture, and they knew the great-great-grandmother I never saw at all, and they laid both these women in narrow pine boxes and sang the same hymns at each graveside. When my mother herself lay dying in her fifty-fourth year, Cecil drove to town every day for six months and sat beside her. He is old now, full of pain, and I never leave his house without wondering if the next time I see him, he may be dressed in his one and only suit, reposing in a store-bought satin-lined casket, his wild head of hair and his grin smoothed down at last by the firm hand of the undertaker's cosmetologist. As I stand with him on the porch, he puts his arm around my neck and holds me against his bony frame, and the clips on his overalls bib clank against my jacket buttons. Rock of Ages, let me hide myself in Thee.

Whom will I ask, when he and Frances are gone, whether great-grandma's hair was straight or curly, and how you make a toothbrush from a sweetgum twig, and what was the name of the sheepdog that saved Mother from the rattlesnake, and how do you butcher a pig and make sausage, and how many kids slept crosswise on each bed those Saturdays twenty relatives came to dinner and decided to spend the night? All of this knowledge will die with him, and when his generation is gone, an essential part of the South will be gone, for he and Frances are truly of the Southern past — made in it and by it. They are our connection with one part of Southern history, that remembrance which, in C. Vann Woodward's phrase, exerts "its perpetual and tragic weight upon the present."

I might have forgotten all this myself except for my Aunt Laura, who though now eighty and living in Oregon, was an eyewitness to many years of Southern history. Many months ago she wrote to ask, "Who are we? What is this special thing we know? Who were these women we remember?" Hoping to make short work of it, I replied that as far as I knew, we came from a line of scrawny old dirt-dobbers, Scotch-Irish with more than one or two Indians thrown in, and that there was no way I could go to the library and read up on Southern country women, let alone our own family, because they didn't make it into the history books.

But that was not enough. She wanted particulars, real things to hold in her hand, real women. She wanted the names and stories. She wanted me to raise the dead. "Who was the first of us?" she asked. "You can track her down." When I protested that I had other things to do and nothing to go on, Laura answered, "Never mind, I'll send you some papers I have. I'll tell you everything I know." And so I began work as an archaeologist might, trying to imagine what a whole village was like by looking at a few pottery pieces in the kitchen midden.

*   *   *

The Southern landscape is gentle in most places, small scale, unthreatening. It cannot match the majesty of other American scenery — the menacing splendor of the Green Mountains under a January blizzard or of the west Texas plains laid out to infinity, shimmering under the August heat. Those are landscapes to die in. The most beautiful part of the South, and the wildest,·is the Appalachians, an ancient mountain range that slices down out of the northeast through Kentucky and Tennessee, finally sloping down toward sea level in Alabama and Georgia. It divides the eastern South from the western like a great stile over a fence.

The Southern mountains are settled down, heavily wooded, rounded off at the corners. Great slow rivers gather on either side of them and roll down toward the Atlantic on the eastern slope and the Mississippi on the western. The lowlands are well watered and lush. Traveling through the South, one is struck by the extravagant colors of the dirt — black, rich brown, burnt orange. Weeds and vines and grass start up and grow at a jungle's pace. Warm weather lasts anywhere from seven to nine months, so nearly anything will take root and sprout. Ironic, that so rich a land has been the nation's poorest part.

It must have looked like paradise to the people who first claimed it. And some of it was. The rice country around Charleston made millionaires. But up from the coast line, in the hills, was treacherous ground. In April came floods, followed by drought in July (the livestock grew scrawny, and the pole beans keeled over, and though the preacher begged the Lord Jesus for rain, the monsoon never came). Nature was unkind, and the hills and rivers full of malevolent things. The Southern woods, even close to the towns, are still filled with croaking, hissing noises. You will be dive-bombed, chewed, punctured, torn, attacked, stung, or turned into a homestead by small creatures that will make you ill, make you itch. In the space of an hour you may see anything from a wildcat to an armadillo. You will have to wear thick boots in case you step on a snake, and you will undoubtedly meet one or two. The most peaceful lake will harbor water moccasins. And as you beat your way through this aggregation of hostile species, the temperature will go up to 100 degrees. Going out in the woods on a summer day gives some idea what the South was like for the people who settled it.

In the beginning, the South was a frontier, perhaps the most intractable and enduring of all American frontiers. In the seventeenth century, it was a toehold along the coasts of Maryland, Virginia, the Carolinas, and Georgia. By 1700, long before anyone had dreamed of a United States, there were some 100,000 settlers on the edge of the rich plain that runs like a wide ribbon down the Atlantic seaboard from Maryland to Georgia. About that time, a few thousand people had begun to beat their way into the tangled, stony interior, up rivers to where the hills rose up, and the rivers rushed over the rocks. By the eve of the American Revolution, they had staked out claims in the Carolina and Virginia back-country and had pressed through the high Appalachian passes into Kentucky and Tennessee. A handful had cut southwestward into the Georgia hills.

They went slowly. They had no ambition to cross the continent, or even the Mississippi — a journey of a hundred miles was enough. Sometimes they went two by two, but more often in small tribes, bands of brothers, sisters, cousins, and other kinfolk. They were all poor people. Most of them, except for a few Germans and French, were the poor of the British Isles — Welsh, Scots, Irish, English, and particularly the Scotch-Irish. They went in wagons, as primitive a set of migrants as any since the Franks and Goths started their slow journey from the Rhineland toward Gaul and Iberia before the Roman Empire fell. Like those other barbarians, these new Southerners owned nothing that wouldn't fit into a wagon — some bedding, perhaps, and a few tin plates and a skillet or two.

They went out into Indian country. If the idea of civilization begins with people living in settled communities not wholly at the mercy of nature, then the Southern Indians were decidedly more civilized than many of these rootless, ignorant Europeans. For by the beginning of the nineteenth century, Southern Indian tribes that had survived the European influx were farmers and villagers. There were five such "Civilized Tribes," as people came to call them: the Cherokees in the Appalachian foothills of Georgia and Tennessee, the Seminoles in Florida, and the Creeks, Chickasaws, and Choctaws in Alabama and Mississippi. Some of them lived in houses, spoke English, understood the basic notions of democracy. Not that civic virtues were to do them much good with Congress in the 1830s when the South decided to seize their lands and drive them permanently across the Mississippi River into Oklahoma.

As the twentieth century began, the South was still, in

places, open country, and the descendants of the migrants who had started from the Carolina back-country were still on the move, trying to lay hold of the rougher regions of Arkansas, Texas, and Oklahoma. If hardship and the will to endure it are what make a frontier, the backward South, from the seaboard to east Texas, retained its frontier culture right up through World War II. Even, in some places, longer. Most Southerners, even those who descend from some distinguished old family or another, can also look back, at quite close range, on at least one line of half-literate farmers who scratched their living out of the dirt one way or another and moved along every generation or so, searching for cheap land and sweet water and the chance to start over again.

That is the invisible Old South, without azaleas or King Cotton or any of the usual props, the vast sector of the antebellum population that had no stake in slavery. In 1860, as the Civil War was about to begin, six million white Southerners, out of a total of eight million, owned no slaves and seldom even set eyes on any. They were farmers or herders or hunters or all three, but whatever they did, not many of them lived in towns. In 1860, New Orleans, with 168,000 people, was the only real city in the South. The North had eight cities larger than New Orleans — New York was already at 800,000 — and the Northern cities were growing. Charleston was an enclave of 40,000, Richmond, 37,000, Nashville, 17,000. The North was already an industrial power, with eighteen and a half million people and 100,000 factories of various kinds. In the South, not even a half million people lived in aggregates of more than 10,000. In 1860, most of these nonslaveholding country people had already been Americans for generations and had already forgotten what year it was that their people had crossed the Atlantic.

These plain people are — presumably — the yeomen that Thomas Jefferson so loved. "Those who labor in the earth," he wrote, "are the chosen people of God, if ever he had a chosen people." Again and again he voiced the idea that

Americans must be a nation of farmers, that its political bedrock would be a sturdy, civic-minded, rural middle class, somehow providing the context against which the upper class bought and sold Negroes. Deeply though he may have loved his yeomen, Jefferson may have misjudged them. For these rural Southerners were not progressives, and some weren't even industrious. What they produced was not for society but for themselves, and they took pride in their own dogged self-sufficiency. If they had to do without schools or stores or markets for their produce, they did without. They did without doctors and lawyers and tried every way they could to do without tax collectors. Civic-minded they were not.

Many people who wrote about them pitied them or hated them — called them poor whites, said that they were victims of the plantation system, forced out of the mainstream of the Southern economy and into the pine barrens. According to this view of things, these farmers themselves aspired to own slaves and live in big white houses but were simply too poor and shiftless to rise up in the world, so they slunk off into the bushes and the high hollows or to some other piece of scruffy real estate and proceeded to make whiskey and get pellagra and commit incest. Dogpatch existed in the newspapers a long time before Al Capp.

But the poor whites were not just benighted hillbillies. They were, on the contrary, the most independent people who ever lived, and I am convinced they went off into the woods of their own will, gladly, by preference, because they believed chiefly in themselves and wanted no truck with institutions. "Wouldn't live in town if they was to give it to me," I heard their great-great-great grandchildren say. The Scotch-Irish, for certain, fled from civilization. They had already had enough of it. The forces that drove them from Ireland to America, and the odds they faced as pioneers in the South, formed the temperament and the attitudes of a certain class of backwoods Southerner for generations.

The term "Scotch-Irish" is not self-explanatory. My mother, whose people were all named Mahaffey and Mc-

Elroy and Moore and Loyd, thought the Scotch-Irish were Scots and Irish who had intermarried, but they were in fact the Ulster Scots, the Northern Irish, the Protestants of a persecuted Catholic country. James I, the first Stuart king of England, had, until the death of his cousin Elizabeth I, ruled Scotland. Elizabeth had been eager to turn Ireland Protestant, to tame it — had, in fact, made a gift of Ulster province to her favorite, the Earl of Essex. Beginning about 1610, James decided to colonize it. He declared that 500,000 acres of land in Northern Ireland were Irish no longer but were open to settlement by Scotsmen and Englishmen. Many of the newcomers crossed the North Channel from western Scotland and settled thereafter in Ulster, in the counties of Down, Tyrone, Derry, Armagh, and Antrim. This was the famous "plantation of Ulster" — the planting of Protestants among Catholics on lands confiscated from the Catholic nobility. These same Protestant counties make up the Republic of Northern Ireland today, attached to England in 1922 by the Anglo-Irish Treaty that set the rest of Ireland free.

In the course of the seventeenth century, the Scots continued to migrate to the northern Irish counties, looking to better themselves and fleeing Scottish misery of all sorts — civil wars and uprisings, the wrath of the English. They came not as conquerors, bearing arms, but as what they were — farmers, weavers, shepherds, laborers, and merchants. They prospered occasionally, in their new homes. By 1641 there were a million and a half of them there. That same year the Irish, who quite understandably hated them, rose up and massacred some 10,000 Ulster Protestants. The English, for their part, slaughtered and exploited both sides. In 1649, Oliver Cromwell marched his Puritan army into Ireland and, to avenge the Ulster massacre, massacred Catholics.

After the Stuart kings were restored, they had but little mercy for the Irish Protestants, whom they regarded as not quite as bad as Catholics, but on the other hand not the right sort of Protestant either. Marriages performed by

Presbyterian clergymen were not legal in the Church of England — to which the Scotch-Irish had to pay tithes. Forbidden by Parliamentary law to seek any market for their beef or wool or other manufactures except in England, the Scotch-Irish were therefore obliged to accept whatever price the English merchants offered — or else starve. They never suffered the way the Catholic peasantry did, but they fit in nowhere. Much of the land they farmed was leased from English landlords, and in 1718, to cite but one year, thousands of leases fell due, and most landlords simply doubled the rents.

No wonder then that by 1720 thousands of Ulster Irish went on their way to America, their numbers swelling from year to year — 10,000 at first, 12,000 next, then 30,000 in a single year. The Catholic Irish would soon follow them, but the Protestants went first. A few went through Boston into New England, but most of them ended up in the Southern backwoods — the hottest tempered, hardest-to-kill, toughest people in the South, according to all accounts of them. Among other talents, they knew how to distill alcohol from barley, and it took a very short time for these new immigrants to adapt the procedure to Indian corn, which yielded a potent whiskey. Not that the Scotch-Irish were invariably drunkards, in spite of the mythic image of the hillbilly with his jug. But with or without a jug, the Scotch-Irish were always on the cutting edge of the westward movement in the South, going through the forest, as historian Bernard Weisberger has described it, like scythes.

I have no idea when my own ancestors arrived. The Scotch-Irish began to migrate in force through the ports of Philadelphia and Charleston about 1720. By now, allowing for ten generations between them and me, there were perhaps five hundred Scotch-Irish ancestors on my mother's side. To try to discover their names would be pointless as well as impossible, but one set of them I know was called McElroy. For the purposes of tracking down the womanly mystique, they'll do as well as any ancestors.

I know they came early. I know they came poor. Maybe

they came as transported prisoners or indentured servants. The first trace of them is in some godforsaken county in the North Carolina back-country in the mid-eighteenth century. Like other new Americans, they came empty-handed, denuded of all possessions except the habits and beliefs they carried in their heads and the Bibles they may or may not have carried. They had no money and no potential as planters, nor, I suspect, any desire to settle down and grow indigo or tobacco or rice in the relatively genteel milieu of the Tidewater. For one thing, they would have hated those Charleston aristocrats in their knee britches — Anglican, lettered, and slavemongering. Even the Presbyterians in Charleston would have been too high-toned. Englishmen, all, too rich to suit the Scotch-Irish. As the McElroys walked hungry and exhausted onto the dock at Charleston harbor, they may have wondered if they would *ever* escape from Englishmen.

Like the blacks, substantial numbers of whom were also being unloaded from ships' holds at about this time, the Scotch-Irish were a people apart. But unlike the blacks, they had a choice about where to go next. They did not linger in the ports or along the shoreline but scuttled immediately away into the backwoods like caged bears suddenly set loose on shore, making their way into a terrifying and savage wilderness where no houses or churches or trading posts or friends stood ready for them — nobody except the Tuscaroras and the Catawbas and the Cherokees — no laws, no courts, no vestige of civil government. There are eyewitness accounts of them landing in America and setting off from the docks the same day, in open boats upriver into the frozen forest, miles away from Charleston. They went with a headstrong resolve that must have been half insane.

To be sure, the citizens of the coastal South, particularly the Charlestonians, were only too eager to send these uncouth and possibly dangerous men and women on their way outside the city limits. The Charleston Assembly had its agents waiting at the docks with land grants, usually tax free for a decade or more, and whatever else the new arriv-

als might need in the way of wagons, horses, tools, and provisions to get on with the journey westward. Personae non
gratae in Charleston, they were desperately needed out in
the back-country (whether they knew it or not) as shock
troops against the Indians — as packhorsemen in case of
war and as traders in times of peace. But more than anything else, they were needed for the color of their skin, to
offset the rapidly rising slave population of the Southern
colonies. With the whites clustered along the coast, there
was nothing to prevent blacks from running away to Indian
country, as many had already done. And. worse than that,
what was to keep the slaves from rising up and killing their
white masters? In September, 1739, on the Stono River just
a few miles south of Charleston, a band of fifty slaves had
staged a desperate, murderous uprising that left the whites
terrified. The essential problem in colonial South Carolina,
as a later historian has observed, was "the Negro problem," that is, the problem of a slave rebellion, and "the
only available remedy was white settlement."

Yet, regardless of whose purposes they unwittingly served,
the new immigrants went on their way voluntarily. Some
of them went without even a wagon, without supplies, and
were seen setting off on foot or with a poor old ghost of a
horse. How could the women consent to go? For these immigrants were young, and many had small, frightened children and were pregnant as well, or carried babies still
nursing. They must have been Indians at heart. An incredulous Charlestonian who went out into the backwoods one
spring to find out whether any of these people had survived
found families living in three-sided lean-tos. They had shot
game all through the freezing weather, and now the women
were planting seed corn, having broken the ground with a
sharp stick.

The books always say that these immigrants wanted land,
and of course they did, but I cannot imagine a greed for
property that would drive men and women out into a lonely
forest, where what they were most likely to run up against
was not a land deed but illness and trouble, maybe death.

And loneliness of a sort that most people are unable to endure. It is contrary to the human survival instinct. Yet some
of them did go for land and wealth. Some even found it
Some of those Scotch-Irish migrants — even a few Mc-
Elroys — became planters and politicians and substantial
citizens of the counties they settled. Some became slaveholders.

In *The Mind of the South,* Wilbur Cash describes with
some malice how a hypothetical backwoods Scotch-Irish-
man can turn into a Southern gentleman in the space of
twenty years. He starts up the social ladder when he sells
his first cotton crop and uses the money to buy a slave.
Next he paints the house white. Then he runs for the legislature. Eventually, in his obituary, the local newspaper
transforms him into an upcountry squire and his widow
into a gentlewoman.

This was not the pattern for most of them. Some stopped
permanently in the high Appalachians or the Georgia hills;
some always moved on. To keep to themselves, they'd have
gone almost off the edge of the earth — not out of any desire to own a piece of it but out of sheer, plain anarchy.
However terrifying the wilderness may have been, something in Belfast and Charleston must have frightened them
more. They and their parents had grown up in a place where
law and order was something that worked against poor
people as often as for them. They loathed all forms of oli-
garchy and to escape it, were all too willing to forego
churches, schools, government, and all other such instruments of torture devised in towns. Somewhere they had
learned that nothing good ever comes out of capital cities,
and their descendants believe that to this day.

So they went out where there were no slaves or indentured servants, no hangmen, no jails, where taxes and fore-
closures and chief magistrates were unheard of. In the wilderness there were no synods, prayer books, nor properly
ordained ministers, nor anything else that European civilization in its wisdom had designed for the likes of them. In
every generation they moved further inland, away from the

sea, and it took the gentry a long time to catch up with their advance guard. As an act of escapism, it was brilliant. "It must have been a magnificent feeling to march down a continent, giving names to town sites and to mountains and streams. That must have marked the start of our real feeling of freedom." So wrote Ben Robertson in *Red Hills and Cotton*, a memoir of his own Scotch-Irish forebears in up-country South Carolina.

And as they went along, they founded a society based not upon currency and commodities but on the elementary notion that if you failed to raise enough to eat, you would go hungry, and if you sheltered the stranger, you might in turn be sheltered by him. But if it turned out that he was too no-account to help you, you got along on your own. It was a wild, breakneck gamble for independence, and for a while it worked.

What must these woman have been like who became partners to such an undertaking? No gentlewomen, certainly, no tenderhearted city girls. For the same gamble that had set the men free did the same for the women. The frontier is one place where a woman is an absolute economic necessity, a full partner in earning the living. Whatever the risks and liabilities of such a life, it must have endowed the women with a certain indisputable equality they could never have bargained out of the devil in County Down. If they had ever been told "because you are a woman you must do this, and you cannot do that," they had at last come to a place where no task would be considered too hard for them and no work too heavy. Travelers who went into the backwoods never failed to comment on the work these women did; "the industrious sex," one observer called them. They plowed and planted and gathered in the wood. They looked after the barnyard animals, fished, and hunted if necessary.

In 1913, in his history of western North Carolina, John P. Arthur, who obviously knew something about women's work, described this day in the life of a Southern frontierswoman:

She "unkivered" the coals which had been smothered in the ashes the night before to be kept alive till morning and with the kindling in one hand and a live coal held in the tines of a fork or between iron tongs in the other, she blew and blew and blew until the splinters caught fire. Then the fire was started and the water brought from the spring, poured into the "kittle" and while it was heating, the chickens were fed, the cows milked, the children dressed, the bread made, the bacon fired, and then coffee was made and the breakfast was ready. That over, and the dishes washed and put away, the spinning wheel, the loom, or the reel were the next to have attention. Meanwhile keeping a sharp lookout for the children and the hawks, keeping the chickens out of the garden, sweeping the floor, making the beds, churning, sewing, darning, washing, ironing, taking up the ashes and making lye, watching for the bees to swarm, keeping the cat out of the milk-pans, dosing the sick children, taping up the hurt fingers and toes, kissing the sore places well again, making soap, robbing the bee-hives, stringing beans for winter use, working the garden, planting and tending a few hardy blossoms in the front yard . . . getting dinner, darning, patching, mending, milking again, reading the Bible, prayers and so on from morning till night and then over again the next day. It could never have been said of them that they had fed on roses and lain in the lilies of life.

But Aunt Laura, pragmatist that she is, wants names. Her own folks. The first McElroy born in America that I can discover and claim as ours is one Isaac, who turns up somewhere in the back-country of the Carolinas in 1763. By that time large numbers of Ulster Scots were living in the backwoods of that region — 400,000 of them along the Cape Fear River alone, near the border between the two colonies. Isaac came from around there, and what I should like to discover, and never shall, is the name of Isaac's mother. How old was she when Isaac was born? Was she born there in the backwoods, or was she instead one of these redoubtable original anarchists who took to the woods as soon as the boat docked? Could she read and write? Card and spin? If she crossed the ocean, had she willingly cut herself free from

Ulster and willingly gone out against such long odds that staying alive could have been all that mattered?

She was my great-great-great-great-grandmother — not just mine, but by now of half the Southern population. I wish I could spend one day with her. Sometimes I imagine her stately and slender on a warm morning, bathing a baby in a creek. I see her hanging his small shirt to dry on a bush. Sometimes I see her ragged and angry, frowzy-headed, contemptuous of soap and water, yelling at her children as she skins a squirrel and hurls the carcass into a gamy, ill-smelling stew.

Occasionally a literate eyewitness journeyed up from the coast and set down his impression of backwoods people, often drawing heroic pictures even when clearly appalled. In 1710, an aristocrat named Phillip Ludwell came across a comparatively well-mannered colonial farm woman: "She is a very civil woman and shews nothing of ruggedness, or Immodesty in her carriage, yett she will carry a gun in the woods and kill deer, turkey &c., shoot down the wild cattle, catch and tye hoggs, knock down beeves with an ax and perform the most manfull Exercises as well as most men in these parts."

Was my great-granny knocking down steers and tying hogs?

Some twenty years later, William F. Byrd II, one of the most enterprising members of his famous Virginia family, went out into the woods to survey the dividing line between his state and North Carolina and, naturally, he kept a diary. He observed, with a mixture of pity and contempt, that the backwoodsmen were "slothful in everything but getting children," and "for all their parts, just like the Indians, impose all the work upon the poor Women. They make their Wives rise out of their beds early in the morning, at the same time that they lye and snore, till the Sun has run one third of his course. . . . Then, after Stretching and Yawning for Half an Hour, they light their Pipes, and under the Protection of a Cloud of Smoak, venture out into the open air. . . ."

The most sympathetic observer of backwoods women was an Anglican divine named Charles Woodmason. His journal is detailed and entertaining and the only one of the period with anything resembling a populist bias or an interest in the female point of view.

The Reverend Mr. Woodmason worked as an itinerant preacher in the Carolina hills for six years, beginning in 1766. It was a violent, savage parish, and what Woodmason says about it shakes up every history-book cliché about the godliness and steadiness of the Bible-toting American pioneer. English by birth and at one time a wealthy planter and slaveholder of Charleston, Woodmason had grown bored with the society of the "sober, sensible, and literate" inhabitants of Charleston, who, as he puts it, "look upon the poor white people in a meaner light than their black slaves." He decided to become an ordained minister of the Church of England and to carry God's law to the frontier. I doubt that the Reverend Woodmason ever ran across my distant grandmother, but I know she must have lived in exactly the same circumstances that this traveling parson so graphically describes.

The conditions of life were appalling, and Woodmason is ever willing to describe his own miseries and those of his straying flock. On New Year's Day, 1767, he writes, "Cross'd the River into the Fork to baptize several Children — A Shocking Passage. Obliged to cut the way thro' the Swamp for 4 miles Thro' Canes, and impenetrable Woods — Had my Cloaths torn to Pieces . . . Went down to St. Marks Church where I officiated on Sunday, Ja. 11, and then returned back to Pine Tree Hill . . . received an Invitation from the People on the Pedee River to visit them . . . where (after many Difficulties — much fatigue, and suffering Hunger, Cold and no Bed to lye on, but only the Ground) I arrived the 22nd."

He has been in the woods since mid-September and notes that he has already traveled 1,300 miles on horseback. The terrain, the discomfort, and the accommodations of January are typical of what he has found among these Southern pioneers — and their cookery, if indeed it can be so called, is, he says, "filthy and most execrable." What provisions they have consist mostly of bacon and cornmeal, and clearly the women have already acquired the habit of drowning everything in grease.

His prospective converts he finds living in a state as execrable as their diet, and their lack of even rudimentary morality stuns him: "For thro' want of Ministers to marry and thro' the licentiousness of the People, many husbands live in Concubinage — swopping their Wives as Cattel, and living in a State of Nature, more irregularly and unchastely than the Indians." He says that North Carolina has no ordained clergymen at all, and reports that large numbers of unlawfully cohabiting couples in North Carolina flock across the border to be wed by him. Yet he is distressed to note that almost every bride he joins in matrimony is "bigg" with child. He attracts gratifyingly large congregations, only to have them get drunk and boisterous before his very eyes.

Woodmason notes that fundamentalists are everywhere — Baptists of every stripe, including New Light and Seventh Day Baptists, freestyle Presbyterians, Dunkards, Quakers. Most of them have barely heard of the Church of England and think it good sport to play rough, lewd jokes upon its representative, such as dressing up in his nightshirt in the dark of the moon and bedding down with some willing woman in his name. They are worse than a pack of woodticks, who are also a source of torment. They are devoid of even the rudiments of religious training or learning. He feels lucky to find anyone who can read the Bible or has even heard of *Pilgrim's Progress*, and they are the prey of robbers and "banditti" of all sorts. "Set down here just as a Barrier between the Rich Planters and the Indians," they are "Without Laws or Government Churches School or Ministers — No Police Established — and all property quite insecure."

But when he gets to the backwoods women, the first thing he mentions is their beauty, and then he complains that they come to church wearing nothing but their "Shifts," barefooted, barelegged, and bareheaded. Yet he is not so displeased with these wild creatures as he wishes he could be. At one point he observes: "The Young Women have a most uncommon Practise, which I cannot break them off. They draw their Shift as tight as possible to the Body, and pin it close, to shew the roundness of their Breasts, and slender Waists (for they are generally finely shaped) and draw their Petticoat close to their Hips to shew the fineness of their limbs — so that they might as well be in Puri Naturalibus — Indeed Nakedness is not censurable or indecent here, and they expose themselves often quite Naked, without Ceremony — Rubbing themselves and their Hair with Bears Oil and tying it up behind them in a Bunch like the Indians. . . ." (I conclude, with some pleasure, that the traditions of rectitude, modesty, and sobriety, which presumably have been handed down among country women since the time of Hengist and Horsa, have a shorter pedigree than I thought.)

But however fine their limbs might be, their lives are harsh: "In many places they have naught but a Gourd to drink out off Not a Plate, Knife or Spoon, a Glass, Cup or anything — It is well if they can get some Body Linen, and some have not even that. They are so burthen'd with Young Children, that the Woman cannot attend both House and Field — and many live by Hunting, and Killing of Deer — There's not a Cabbin but has 10 or 12 Young Children in it — When the Boys are 18 and Girls 14 they marry — so that in many Cabbins You will see 10 or 15 Children. Children and Grand Children of one size — and the Mother looking as Young as the Daughter. Yet these poor People enjoy good health. . . ."

Some of what Woodmason describes is simply the fertility and destitution of the Scottish and Irish and English peasantry in the mid-eighteenth century: the ills of the old country transported, pretty much intact, to its new colonies. For it was around 1750 that what we now call the "population explosion" began. Travelers in the British Isles at that period, for example, regularly describe the stark but fecund little dwellings where a dozen or more half-naked children would fatten on oats or potatoes one year and die of starvation the next — for good and sufficient reasons that the Reverend Thomas Robert Malthus would set down on paper before the eighteenth century ended. Malthus, in *An Essay on the Principle of Population*, proclaimed the dark theory that death by malnutrition was one sure result of human fecundity. Like Woodmason, he too was a country parson who had to baptize and bury the children of the overly fruitful rural poor.

But Woodmason's burgeoning populations, unlike Malthus's, would live to see their lives improved. In time the anarchy of the Carolina backwoods would diminish. After the Revolutionary War, some tentative form of government would appear there — a few jails for the banditti, a few courthouses and sheriffs and clerks. Some of the children swarming in those wretched cabins would grow up and dig the stumps out of the land that the first generation had claimed. Others would simply pack up and move on, taking little with them and leaving little behind.

And so it was with Isaac McElroy, that pre-Revolutionary frontier child, for in 1785 he and a passel of his brothers turned up in the Georgia hill country. He was twenty-five that year and had a wife and a land grant, which no doubt was given for some piece of soldiering in the war. He left his birthplace and moved along, and by 1800 the census shows Scotch-Irish all over Oglethorpe County, which is where they first settled down. Georgia was by no means to be their last stop — Isaac, for example, moved farther west in Georgia, and didn't quit until he died in western Alabama.

By the time Isaac McElroy and his brothers were settling down in Georgia, Isaac's mother was no doubt dead. At any rate, nowhere in the meager records can I find evidence that she went along to Georgia. She was my primal female ancestor, the only one that I can conjure up even in a tenuous, spectral, and anonymous form.

I imagine her arising in her drafty cabin on a winter

morning, making her way among the slumberers around the hearth. She uncovers the live coals under the ashes, adds some kindling, blows at the flame. She wraps a shawl around her and goes to the cowshed, returning with a panful of foaming milk. Then she stirs up hoecakes, flat and tough enough to chip the teeth of the Reverend Woodmason or anyone else. I am willing to admit that she may have been a terrible cook. Most of the women in my family have hated cooking, preferring to be outside in the sun, and I suppose the tradition began early. I see her chopping long rows of corn, digging the sweet-potato patch. Is she cursing her husband, who lies abed or sits at the doorway blowing smoke rings? I see her sunning herself on a rock, yearning for a mirror as she coats her brick-brown Scotch-Irish hair with bear oil and ties it up in a bunch behind her head like an Indian. Off she goes on her way to the preaching, pulling her shift up under her breasts and pinning up her petticoat to display her fine figure. (My ancestresses have all had fine figures and have never objected to showing them off. My mother and aunt once roused their father's wrath by going off to church in tight, short, red-and-white dresses that they had made themselves. Granddad made them cut the dresses up into quilt scraps.)

I can never lift the obscurity that keeps me from knowing the dates of her birth and death or the shape of her face or her name. (Was it Catora? Catherine? Birdie? Those names have been handed down.) But I will not explain her away as an embarrassing backwoods aberration or turn her into the proper calico-clad frontier heroine of my schoolbooks. I am not ashamed of her for being poor or ragged or dirty nor would I ever believe that the exigencies of the frontier brutalized her. Even if she could not read and went barefoot, even if she didn't know the proper liturgical responses in church and went off to holler and jump with the New Light Baptists, I would rather have her for my ancestor than all the ladies of Charleston. Maybe she smoked a pipe or dipped snuff or pulled a plow or in other ways failed to live up to the womanly ideal. In my library full of books and my manuals of Southern tombstones, land deeds, and ships' manifests, I cannot discover that anyone, in all her life, ever bothered to write down her name, so I cannot write it down for her. But I can write that I honor her, if that is not too small a tribute and too late, and that something of what she was and what she did has been passed down from generation to generation and endures.

Three

Drowned Women

The disintegration of a culture is a melancholy event. If I grew up in the simple-minded belief that women were as strong and intelligent as men, it was because I came from a society that had once believed it. But as I rake around for proof of that belief, I realize that I am almost too late. Elderly aunts, for those fortunate enough to have them, are a formidable resource. What they can do, if they wish, is to forge a chain of remembrance. They can offer bits of cake soaked in tea, as Marcel Proust's great-aunt did on certain afternoons, bits of madeleine that years afterward, on other afternoons, will open up a path to some remote region of the brain, calling up what we thought was gone or had failed to realize was there — knowledge to link us to the world's beginnings.

Aunt Laura is four thousand miles away and would not indulge me in madeleines and *infusions* even if she could, but many months ago, she sent me such history as she had. A few letters, spelled out in her laddery, painful penmanship, an old photograph, and a copy of a census taker's handiwork, dated 1880, from Lafayette County, Mississippi. All this is at first cryptic and unyielding to me — a picture, a list, and an octogenarian's scattershot recollections of days so distant that she is now the only living witness. The census page records the names of a young farmer and his wife and children — and a few miscellaneous facts about their ancestry — who lived on a tract of land near Oxford, Mississippi, the county seat. I manage to summon up the intelligence that this is William Faulkner's county. Yoknapatawpha County, 1880. Tillman and Eliza McElroy, aged twenty-seven and twenty-six, with three small children and a couple of their relations living with them besides. Dirt farmers. Are they the Snopes family? The photograph, which was taken in Arkansas nineteen years later, shows the same family that the census page enumerates, but vastly increased. Well, whatever their reproductive proclivities, at least they don't look like Faulknerian poor folks.

None of this is quite so exquisite as biscuits dipped in tea, and the visions evoked by these utterly commonplace bits of the past — though they are, curiously enough, contemporaneous with Proust's visions — are ludicrous by comparison. A mansion in a lovely village of the Ile-de-France, against a log house in northern Mississippi. Women with lace on their dresses, a servant in the kitchen caverns stripping asparagus stalks, a darkened bedroom upstairs where a sickly little boy lies and frets, as against this work-roughened crew in the picture, who never lived in a house with a staircase, never had a servant, never heard of asparagus, or got farther above the rocky soil than the hayloft in their barn or the top of a tree or a mule's back.

I examine the old picture as if I were a lepidopterist with a hitherto unclassified specimen of butterfly. Made in 1899 it is the oldest, in fact the only, surviving photograph of this Southern frontier family. It must resemble a million other such photographs. It is not of stunning quality — nothing for the Museum of Modern Art. If I had found it in an old box or at the back of a drawer, I could hardly have looked at it. But now I bend over it, with Laura's questions in my head, and I try to summon up what I know — stories

I used to hear at funerals and family reunions, the epic poetry of a people who knew little about history, did not read books, did not keep diaries. Who are we? Where did we come from? And what can be said about the women in this picture?

There are twenty-one people counting the babies. They have come outdoors for the picture taking: they pose against a background of scrub pine. Even on so great an occasion as this — the first time any of them had ever been photographed? — they are totally lacking in finery. They all look scrubbed, and the men wear vests and ties. Only one of the women has any sort of ornament, and it is a miniscule brooch worn by the oldest and most imposing woman in the picture, Eliza Moore McElroy. There she sits in the middle of them all, in the last June of the nineteenth century, her hands folded calmly in her lap, her face composed, but her eyes anxious. She is a sturdy soul in the midst of her children and grandchildren, who look able-bodied, scrappy, and bright. All the children are barefoot. Everybody is young: using the birth dates on the census, I quickly conclude that no one in the three generations can be older than twenty-five except Tillman and Eliza, who are in their mid-forties. Today they would hardly qualify as middle-aged.

They have the good looks and dignity of a pair of hand-turned, homemade kitchen chairs. Eliza's hair is skinned back; she is no beauty, but Tillman is mountain king, with a bib of thick, curly beard that conceals his shirt collar and lapels. They are the parents not only of the four-year-old boy clutching Tillman's hand but of the hale and smiling young woman seated at far left holding her infant twins and clutched on either side by another son and daughter. And between the youngest and the eldest, Eliza bore twelve other children, two of whom died in infancy. She was a grandmother before her last son was born. In all of this she is a woman of her time, perhaps luckier than most to have buried only two.

Across the world in London, possibly on this same day,

Queen Victoria sat for her photograph, grumpy and jowly, Empress of India, grandmother of Europe. The flash powder exploded discreetly, preserving the titled head forever, like a peach pickled in brandy. Everything that Victoria said and did in June, 1899, has been carefully set down. It is all there. One could write a volume about how Queen Victoria spent the month of June that year. But here is Eliza Moore McElroy, admitted to history just as much as the Queen by that most democratic of all political instruments, the camera. Very little was entered in the record about her, however, besides a note on the reverse: "Tillman and Eliza McElroy and children. Garland County, Arkansas June, 1899. Twins in Mama's arms born March 4, 1899."

"Mama," holding her twins, is the eldest McElroy child, Lavisa Eugenia. She lived in an epoch skilled at working its womenfolk to death and at twisting their minds and bodies in corsetry of every kind. Yet she looks wonderfully unfettered. Her face glows with energy, her shoulders are wide, and in her eyes is a gleam of readiness. More often than not, farm women in old photographs like this look worn out and desperate. In the Southern backwoods, God knows, lived many a tobacco-stained crone, old at forty and bowed down by toil, featureless under a floppy sunbonnet. But here sits Lavisa Eugenia, straight as a pine tree, ready to do battle with anything that turns up.

Lavisa, people always said, was an Indian name — they said it LaVYsie. Eugenia, Eugénie, had been the name of an Empress of France who was still alive in 1874 when this namesake of hers was born in the Mississippi sticks. (The name for a first-born daughter is always compounded from fantasies and bestowed as magic. Unconsciously, the mother commands, "Live up to this name." I wonder how Eliza came up with such a combination.)

Lavisa is twenty-five in the photograph, a recent widow and the mother of four. She looks capable of bearing her bereavement. On each palm, she balances an infant son, making sure that his face will show up for the camera. Her great square hands are ample for cradling the bottoms of three-month-old twins. Beside her stand a son of about five, whose thin arm lies across his mother's shoulders as he smiles nervously for the photographer, and a little girl of three with her hair in sausage curls, her frame enveloped in an enormous dress that hangs down to her incongruous bare toes — Laura, the sole survivor.

Back in Mississippi, when she was about eighteen, Lavisa had married a man named Ras Mahaffey, "Razz," and old-fashioned, countrified name. They had packed up whatever possessions they had and had gone homesteading in Indian territory, Choctaw country, in fact, near a frontier town in eastern Oklahoma called Poteau. In the 1890s the Bureau of Indian Affairs had finally got around to settling the claims of the the Mississippi Choctaws, the pitiful and dying hand-ful that had remained in Mississippi after their brethren had been carried off to Oklahoma. Half a century passed; now at last reparations were to be made. Anybody with proof of Choctaw ancestry could claim a farm out there in the desolation. Ras Mahaffey qualified. But homesteading was a high-risk occupation, and his claim turned out to be his grave.

He left his widow with a son and daughter and pregnant with the twin boys, alone in a sod house on the verge of winter. There she stayed until the sons were born next spring. She had no one to look to but herself. Who came, I wonder, to help at the birth? Surely the Widow Mahaffey had neighbors, and surely they helped her out occasionally. Did they bring food to her door or stop long enough to draw a few buckets of water from the well for her or bring it up from the spring? While she nursed her twins, did they tell a story or two to Laura and her brother, desolate without their father and now saddled with two squalling baby brothers? Who made the beds, washed the clothes, milked the cow, took up the butter from the churn? Did the chil-dren cry all night, the twins hungry and the older ones afraid, so that their mother never rested?

Laura cannot remember. But she can recall her mother weeping on the journey back to Arkansas, for she did finally give up and go home. "We came part way on the train. The windows were open, and the soot blew on us. Whenever the whistle blew, so lonely, Mama would think about Papa and begin to cry," writes Laura. Her memories come back to her in the nighttime, in dreams. Of the earlier months she recalls only that "Mama loved us. We were never cold or hungry. She always cared for us." And after they had returned to the comparative comfort of the McElroy homestead, she soon moved her family to a log house on a forty-acre farm nearby, an independent woman looking after what she had. No one forbade her to do as she pleased. "Ain't you afeard to stay by yourself at night, sister?" they might have asked, and she surely smiled and said no.

What broke her down and stayed the motion of those square hands was the death of her twins. When they were six, those little boys went out in the woods, ate poisonous berries, and came back to die in their mother's arms. She buried them and, unable to endure living in the house where this terrible event had happened, went home once more. After a while she got married again, this time to a thriving widower named Andy Loyd who had five children of his own; he and Lavisa produced five more, including another pair of twins, one of whom was Velma, my mother. Lavisa's last child was born when she was forty-four. Then she grew old, a benevolent presence clad in a sunbonnet and a flowered dress. I can recall sitting on her lap, her bony chest against my head, the dark skin of her face stretched from cheekbone to cheekbone like a cured hide. She never had much to say, never told stories about her heroic past. Bound as she was to an ancient code of conduct, she lived relentlessly in the present. Today's bread was to bake. Yesterday's did not matter. The earliest coherent memory of my childhood is of watching her coffin go down into the red earth and hearing cries of grief at her graveside.

Leisure was a word unknown to her. She never did anything merely for the exercise or worried about her weight (she was always thin, but it wouldn't have mattered either way). She would no more have put cosmetics on her face than she would have painted her house and barn. Hospitals and drugstores were unknown to her — she never dosed herself with anything that she had not gleaned from the woods and brewed herself. A good soaking in coal oil was what she recommended for all kinds of wounds. (My mother believed in coal oil, too, and only my father's volubly expressed Yankee scorn rescued me from such remedies. He himself believed in mercurochrome.) Teething pains in a baby, Lavisa thought, could be eased by taking a thimble and running it gently over the child's gums: such notions would, of course, occur to a woman looking after a baby and doing ten other jobs at once. Whatever the needs of the people under her roof, she saw to them. If twenty-five people turned up on a Saturday night, as often happened, and announced they'd come to stay a week, she shook out the feather tickings and stoked up the cookstove.

She never lay in bed past daybreak, even when she was sick. The running of the house, the tending of the livestock, and the growing and preserving of food were wholly in her care. She worked in the fields, if necessary, plowed and planted, set fence posts, raked hay. She was, according to witnesses, an administrator. The responsibilities of baby care and housework she rapidly passed on to the eldest children, who began to assume their duties as cooks and dishwashers and baby tenders by the time they were five or six. For this reason, perhaps, she was never heard to complain that children were a burden. There were usually a dozen dependents in her household, and I know that although her young 'uns sometimes went off to school ragged or in ill-fitting shoes, the rags were clean and ironed, and the bellies full. She accomplished all this largely without machinery, except in her early years a spinning wheel and loom, and later a treadle sewing machine. Her daily rounds took her close to cranky animals, boiling cauldrons of fat or water, scythes and axes, redhot stoves, but though she knew a great deal about injury and pain and death, she knew nothing of violence.

In public she and her husband, Andy Loyd, addressed

each other with the honorific and the surname, and for all
I know called one another Mr. and Mrs. in bed. Their respect for one another was palpable. She never needed to
ask his permission about anything, and she knew as much
about running the farm as he did. Never, in the middle of
her life, did the corrosive suspicion descend upon her that
all her work had been pointless and her achievements neg-
ligible. Menopause to her meant simply the end of bearing
children, and I should think she welcomed it. But when that
last one was born to her, in her forty-fourth year, a "change
baby," she loved him almost more than the rest, and he
grew up to be the sunniest and heartiest of the lot.

Lavisa Eugenia's life stretched almost from Appomattox
to the beginning of World War II, but grand events meant
nothing to her. She had an inbred independence from anything that happened outside Garland County. Though she
had produced treasure for the world, in the form of self-
sufficient children, crops for the market, food for the table,
cloth woven and thread spun, souls prayed into salvation,
she took almost nothing from society in return. She never
paid any taxes, but I don't suppose that one tax dollar was
ever laid out on her behalf, unless one counts the stingy bit
allotted to country schools in those days. Money was of no
importance to her. Nor did she ever require the service of
professionals: nothing that needed doing was beyond her.
When she died, her friends made her a coffin and dug her
a hole in the ground. She was one of the last of the Scotch-
Irish loners and fugitives. I know that she loved and hon-
ored her husbands, both of them, but if necessary, as she
had proved, she could survive alone in a wilderness. She
did not live to see her granddaughters as grown women. I
wonder what she might have said about our various heart-
aches and vexations.

* * *

The woman who raised such daughters as this was Eliza
Moore McElroy. Even in the skeletal facts of her life that
survive, she stands as a kind of astonishing corrective to a

large swatch of the mythological South. She was born, "borned" she would have said, in a log house in northern Mississippi in 1853, the daughter of a pair of migrants who had come from around the North Carolina-Tennessee border, journeying westward in a wagon over the Natchez Trace. This was the famous bandit-ridden wilderness path that was more an Indian trail than a road. When or why they came or who they were is forever undiscoverable. They were Scotch-Irish, but their daughter's face is testimony enough that their lineage was not wholly Celtic. In her photograph at the age of forty-five, Eliza is unmistakably an Indian — part Cherokee was how the legend usually ran, though without any proof in particular.

With proof or without it, during the last thirty years of her life Eliza's countenance changed into an Indian mask, leathery and swarthy, the eyes sunken, the cheekbones jutting outward like elbows, the lips tucked in tightly across her teeth. This look engraved itself, in many variations, on the features of several of her descendants. (At a funeral some time ago, an old man came up to say hello and shake my hand, and though I could not recall ever seeing him before, and knew Eliza only from her picture, I instantly recognized him as kinfolk, for he wore her Indian face.) It is more than the dark complexion, however, and the broad facial architecture. It is also a kind of bitter snap in the eye that recurs with the regularity of a recessive gene. "That damned, insolent hillbilly look," my father used to call it, but I don't think it came from hillbillies.

The Southern Indians are submerged in a stratum of historical invisibility even more obscure than the one reserved for blacks. Charles M. Hudson, a current authority on Southern Indians, believes that we have "a virtual amnesia about the parts of our past in which they are involved." In our selective memory, there is only one Indian in Southern history — Pocahontas. She had a famous encounter, or nonencounter, as the case may be, with Captain John Smith near Jamestown. She saved the Captain from her father's wrath, or so he said. Then she married John Rolfe, another

Englishman, and lived just long enough to produce a son by him. Among the genealogically minded, it is the supreme honor to trace one's roots back to this particular mixed marriage. But there were other Indians, too, less remote and much less acceptable socially. And there were other white connections with them, too.

None of this, of course, is of any genetic consequence. Nor does it matter to the few Cherokees or Choctaws who manage today to hang onto their tribal identity. But it does go against a cherished piece of Southern conventional wisdom — the lunatic old myth of racial purity, that piece of self-delusion that takes pride in the absence of foreign names and alien blood in the South. Nobody here but us circumspect white folks, as far back as the eye can see. This notion has never stood up very well where black people are concerned, since large numbers of them have white ancestry. (No one knows how many: scholarly estimates go as high as 75 per cent. Nor are there any figures, obviously, on whites with black ancestry.)

But until a remarkably late date, the South was not only biracial but triracial. In the seventeenth and eighteenth centuries, the colonists in the Tidewater efficiently exterminated the coastal tribes, such as the Catawbas and the Tuscaroras (or took them as slaves). However, the tribes of the interior not only survived but flourished well into the nineteenth century. The Cherokees, whose native land was the Appalachians, fought on the British side during the Revolutionary War, but once they perceived where the future lay, they made peace and settled back into their customary agrarian ways. They were far too intelligent to imagine that the newly formed United States would simply go away and let them be, so they decided, as a defeated power, to apply for technological aid. "Ploughs, hoes, cattle and other things for a farm, this is what we want," said the Cherokee chief at the signing of the peace treaty in 1791. "We desire you to assist us."

Farming was not new to the Cherokees; the women, in particular, had always been experts at it. The classic Indian triad, corn, beans, and squash, was what they raised. Like other eastern American tribes, they also gathered wild produce, and the men hunted. No one knows much about them before historical times, but they were part of a vast, well-organized culture with democratic political traditions. They were accustomed to village life, and by the time the South began to move westward into their country, at the beginning of the nineteenth century, the Cherokees were close to being assimilated American farmers — poor, of course, but no more than the average frontiersman. However, by that time, the Cherokee domain had shrunk ominously. Thirty years after the signing of the treaty, the Cherokee homeland had been stripped down to several thousand acres in the mountainous region where Tennessee, Georgia, North Carolina, and Alabama come together.

Still, they managed. The typical dwelling there was a frame house, not a tepee. The Cherokees were literate by then, for in 1821, their chief, Sequoya, perfected a syllabary, an ingenious method for writing down his people's language. (He was the legitimate son of a rich Kentuckian named Nathaniel Gist and a Cherokee noblewoman.) By that time the Cherokees knew at least as much about law and order as their backwoods neighbors. They had become a self-governing republic with a constitution and a democratically elected legislature. From their capital at New Echoba, Georgia, they even published a bilingual newspaper which was distributed nationally. By 1825, all but about five percent of them lived on single-family farms. They owned plows, looms, spinning wheels, and wagons; had their own blacksmithies, cotton gins, and gristmills. A few of them even qualified as honest-to-God Southern gentlemen, for their upper echelon had taken to raising cotton and owning slaves.

Of all the Civilized Tribes, the Cherokees were probably the most apt at absorbing the culture of the European, but the Creeks in Alabama, the Choctaws in Mississippi, and even the once-ferocious Chickasaws had also taken up Christianity and metallurgy and chosen educated men as their chiefs. All hoped that they might be allowed to stay where they were. (The Seminoles in Florida, alone among the five tribes, were not anxious to join up with white America. Seminole country had always been a refuge for fugitive slaves, who, if they could manage to cross the south Georgia border and reach an Indian village, were usually adopted as tribesmen. By the early nineteenth century, the Seminoles were virtually a black nation. So long as Spain held the peninsula, they were safe. But the slaveholders of Georgia, in particular, hated them.)

All this has mostly been forgotten, along with its corollary, which is that it was not simply a question of wild Indians turning themselves into white people, but white Southerners in some sense turning into Indians, as well. On the frontier, at least in the seventeenth and eighteenth centuries, there had to be some common ground between Indians and settlers. Otherwise the settlers could never have survived. Whether friendly Indians dropped in on their new neighbors and gave them lessons in agronomy is dubious, but the settlers, somehow or other, had to Indianize. They arrived as often as not totally ignorant of planting and harvesting and accustomed to the barley, oats, and mutton that had been the basis of life in the British Isles since Roman times. Now they had to learn to depend on corn, raising it by the Indian method of interplanting squash, pumpkins, and beans — all of which, except for the beans, would have been strange to them.

All this new knowledge definitely fell into the women's sphere. So did the cooking. Somehow, backwoods women learned to cook like Indians, taking the corn and grinding it with stones, frying it into flat cakes, baking it into thin loaves, turning it into hominy, mush, or grits, laying the ripe, roasting ears under the coals to cook in their shucks, drying the tough beans and field peas of late summer, and stewing them for hours in a pot, then seasoning them with animal fat. (The Indians liked bear and squirrel grease; the settlers preferred pig.) All these classic ingredients and methods of Southern cooking were Indian ways, as was the habit of searching the woods for wild vegetables, berries, and herbs — ginseng, sassafras, poke sallet, muscadines, hickory nuts, mint. And the women also learned to butcher and cook Indian game — the wild turkeys and groundhogs, possums, rabbits, deer. Besides its content and methods, the cuisine devised by squaws and hillbilly women, as well as slave women, had another thing in common, which was the belief that you made do with whatever you could lay hands on — pigs' entrails, turnip tops, cowpeas, terrapins, catfish — anything that didn't bite you first.

How these exchanges were made no one knows. There were no sociologists out in the woods taking notes on cultural crosscurrents, and if whites and Indians married and settled down to live as American citizens outside Indian boundaries, the fact was seldom recorded. Indians and whites did marry, of course, so often that Cherokees had to devise elaborate laws on the subject of interracial marriages. These forbade whites and Cherokees to cohabit without the formality of a marriage license and a legal ceremony and prohibited a white man from having both a white and an Indian wife. Whites married to Cherokees were afforded full citizenship in the Cherokee nation, but Indian wives retained their property rights. The Cherokee census of 1835 showed that, out of a population of 16,000, fully a fourth were mixed bloods, and at that moment 200 white men and women were residents and citizens of the Nation by virtue of their duly recorded marriages to Cherokee husbands or wives.

In the end, of course, it made no difference. Literate or not, legally wed or not, civilized or savage, the Southern Indians were all uprooted in the late 1830s and herded to Oklahoma like animals. A new order of politician had taken control in Georgia and Tennessee and Mississippi, and after the election of Andrew Jackson they had a powerful ally in Washington. These men wanted the Indians removed. The Cherokee leadership, under the direction of their president, John Ross, lobbied desperately in Washington against removal. But the Southerners had their way. Congress set the month of May, 1838, as the last date when any Cherokee could live east of the Mississippi. That month five regiments of U.S. Army regulars and 4,000 militiamen, under General Winfield Scott, arrived in Cherokee country, and the roundup began.

Many years later a report was submitted to the Bureau of Ethnology in Washington by James Mooney, who went to Oklahoma after the removal and interviewed survivors.

> Squads of troops were sent to search out with rifle and bayonet every small cabin hidden away in the coves or by the sides of mountain streams, to seize and bring in as prisoners all the occupants, however or wherever they might be found. Families at dinner were startled by the sudden gleam of bayonets in the doorway and rose up to be driven with blows and oaths along the weary miles of trail that led to the stockade. Men were seized in their fields or going along the road, women were taken from their wheels and children from their play. In many cases, on turning for one last look as they crossed the ridge, they saw their homes in flames, fired by the lawless rabble that followed on the heels of the soldiers to loot and pillage. . . . A Georgia volunteer, afterward a colonel in the Confederate service, said: "I fought through the civil war and have seen men shot to pieces and slaughtered by thousands, but the Cherokee removal was the cruelest work I ever knew."
> To prevent escape the soldiers had been ordered to approach and surround each house, so far as possible, so as to come upon the occupants without warning. One old patriarch, when thus surprised, calmly called his children and grandchildren around him, and kneeling down, bid them pray with him in their own language, while the astonished onlookers looked on in silence. Then, rising, he led the way into exile. A woman, on finding the house surrounded, went to the door and called up the chickens to be fed for the last time, after which, taking her infant on her back and her two other children by the hand, she followed her husband with the soldiers.

The mortality rate along the Trail of Tears was genocidal. Of the 17,000 Cherokees rounded up, at least 4,000 died in the six-month-long march from Georgia to Oklahoma. Those who lived found themselves in a barren, intemperate plain without shelter, tools, or resources.

But as with all acts of gross destruction, there are invariably a few cracks and interstices where people can hide. (Even in Berlin in the 1940s some 2,000 Jews survived at large until the end of World War II, and though the politicians and militiamen of the South may have had some of the inclinations of Nazis, they were nowhere near as systematic.) Most of the Cherokees were taken unawares, unable to comprehend the monstrous thing that was about to be done to them; even as General Scott arrived in Georgia, John Ross was still in Washington, pleading for a stay of execution, and many Cherokees may have held on, immobilized. But there had to be a few who ducked out of the holocaust.

All this took place some fifteen years before Eliza was born. Her parents might have been children during the Cherokee removal and by all rights should have been hauled off to Oklahoma with the rest of their kind, in which case Eliza McElroy might never have existed. But there she is in Arkansas in 1899 with her Indian face. Perhaps her parents were among the small band of Cherokees that escaped into North Carolina; perhaps they were an Indian-Scotch-Irish couple living on the frontier. Or perhaps they escaped from their captors and ran away to Mississippi. Not many Cherokees, according to the scholars, managed to penetrate the white world. And yet the traces of them are there — in the kitchen and the garden, if nowhere else.

If there is such a thing as an Indian heritage among Southern women, a legacy that amounts to more than hoecakes and bone structure, or even that damned, insolent look in the eye that so unnerved my father, it would have to belong to the people of the backwoods. I imagine that it may show itself in a certain cynicism that, in my family at least, runs through the political attitudes of the women like a fine seam of coal. One thing that they taught me was that politicians are the source of all disillusionment.

If Eliza had been alive in 1957, she would have known, as my mother knew, just what Orval Faubus was up to in Little Rock, or Lester Maddox or George Wallace, in their respective capitals. I fondly picture a long line of these country girls, back through the years, poking fun at Cotton Ed Smith, Tom Watson, Senator Vardaman, and all that sorry breed who specialize in playing the redneck off against the black and then double-crossing both. (They pose, invariably, as defenders of white wives and daughters.) God knows these women could have learned these attitudes easily enough without having them handed down from some Indian ancestress. But the disillusion of the Cherokees would have married up nicely with the old Scotch-Irish anarchism: the suspicion that whatever your color or creed may be, when you get too close to civilization, you can probably expect to be done in.

* * *

Like her daughter Lavisa, Eliza was no storyteller or diary keeper. She was a little girl when the Civil War began, old enough to have witnessed and remembered some of the more brutal events that occurred in and around Oxford, Mississippi. No one can recall her ever saying a word about any of it, and I cannot be sure what she saw or thought. But she cannot have ignored it. The tragic absurdities of what she would have observed cannot have escaped even an eight-year-old child.

Oxford, in the 1850s, was a village with a few unpaved streets and not quite 4,000 inhabitants. It is not much more than a village today, but it has taken on the quality of an antique and holy Southern place, with its lovely white Victorian courthouse and its literary sanctification as the home of William Faulkner and the locus of his novels. But in Eliza's time, it was the Wild West — a raw town hastily thrown together. (Before 1833, as Faulkner himself wrote, it was nothing but "one long rambling onestorey mudchinked log building housing the Chickasaw Agent and his tradingpost store.") Lafayette County, which was carved out of the

Chickasaw cession of 1836, had attracted a large number of settlers — farmers and frontiersmen mostly, though there were some planters and slaveholders as well. The name chosen for the new town was no fluke — Oxford's founder intended that the state university would be established there, and his wish was eventually granted, after a bitter brawl in the state legislature in Jackson, where the sentiment ran toward putting the school in the delta, closer to the money and the potential consumers of higher learning, who were scarce enough in Mississippi, even down around Natchez.

In 1848, though there was not so much as one public school in all of Mississippi, not one place where a child of poor parents could learn to read and write, Ole Miss opened its doors, which were rather elaborate doors, considering the time and place. Its central hall was a multicolumned Greek Revival pile known as the Lyceum, and there were some dormitories and faculty houses as well. The purpose of the school was to knock some culture into rich men's sons. And if the local population had heard any talk about genteel plantation manners and the pretty ways of cavaliers, the student body must have taken them completely by surprise.

They rode to school on horseback with plenty of whiskey, guns, hunting dogs, and black servants, and apparently not the remotest aptitude for philosophy or belles-lettres or astronomy or anything else the faculty proposed to teach them. They hunted and drank and thought up practical jokes. The habits of the freshman class of 1848 were such that by midterm the university president decided to flee back east in the middle of the night, without notice, and more than half the freshmen had either been expelled for drunkenness or had merely dropped out. Deportment among the scholars did not improve in the next decade. As the fever for war grew hotter in the late 1850s, the students took to tormenting slaves in town and in the neighboring countryside, beating, branding, terrorizing. At length they made such a menace of themselves that three of them were actually brought to trial for rape (the victim was a black maid in the new president's household). Nothing was done to them.

Country folks probably tried to stay out of the way of these young aristocrats and to keep their unprintable opinions to themselves. In April, 1861, after the firing on Sumter, every student at Ole Miss was mustered into the Confederate Army — as the University Grays — in a large and noisy ceremony in the town, after which they clattered off toward Jackson, whooping like Indians, according to a witness. (The rebel yell, in fact, is supposedly an imitation of the Chickasaw war cry, yet another Indian heritage besides cornbread and cynicism). A great and no doubt delighted crowd gathered to watch them go. It is quite likely that Eliza, a barefoot farm girl in homespun, was among the onlookers.

Her father and her older brothers would soon be in the army, too, angry, unwilling conscripts with nothing to gain and no idea what they were fighting for, except to defend their homesteads, which they could have better defended from the front porch. However, according to a law that had just been passed by the legislature in Jackson, any man with more than twenty slaves was exempt from military service, while farmers with no slaves were required to go out and die. If any orator that day exhorted them to join up and fight for the Southern way of life — a noble cause involving the institution of slavery and the honor of those young gentlemen galloping southward — the crowd would surely have laughed.

The fortitude of upper-class Southern women during the Civil War is one of the sacrosanct themes in the mythology of the region: Great-granny defying those blue-coated sons-of-bitches under the portico, just after she had personally buried the sterling silver and put down a small mutiny among the field hands. The backwoods women (lacking any such melodramatic props) had little to be heroic about. I don't suppose Eliza and her mother felt heroic as they, and the wives and daughters of thousands of men at the front, plowed their land alone for the next four springs. As the older women took on the work of men, children like Eliza did the work of women, following down the furrows, dropping seed corn into the ground, milking the cows, skimming the cream and churning, sweeping the floors and the front yard every morning, starting the fire and laying the fatback in the skillet. But hardship set in quickly: the Confederate commissariat was far more terrifying to the country people than the Federal Army. Eliza's workload was no doubt occasionally lightened by the arrival of officials who rounded up the poultry and cattle and herded them down the road toward Oxford.

And if Eliza had learned to love a few of the luxuries of civilization by then — little papers of steel pins and needles, wheat flour to make biscuits, oil for a lamp, paper, ink, coffee, an orange at Christmastime, she soon found that all these had completely vanished from the general store in town, and soon the people of the backwoods would be reduced to the harsh conditions their grandparents had faced in the forests of North Carolina and Kentucky. For children like Eliza, the only lasting gift of the Confederacy was to be this war and the unending desolation it induced.

Exactly a year after the University Grays rode off, 77,000 Rebel and Union troops met at Shiloh, in Tennessee, about eighty miles northeast of Oxford. The result was a classic Civil War disaster, not a battle so much as a communal massacre of confused and pitifully untrained men, most of whom had never before fired a rifle. Nevertheless, they murdered one another very capably. Fully a third of them were dead or wounded when the fracas ended. The beaten Confederates backtracked out of Tennessee into Mississippi; cartloads of wounded and dying men bounced down the long roads into the village of Corinth, which soon had to be abandoned, and then on to Oxford, where the colonnaded Lyceum had been turned into a hospital. Perhaps Eliza stood by the roadside, watching and listening. Perhaps she went to the university and looked through a window at the shattered young men from Illinois, Ohio,

Tennessee, and Mississippi — eyeless, jawless, legless — laid out on hard cots or even on the floorboards until they died of shock or gangrene. Like all Confederate hospitals, this one was simply a place to stack bodies. The only surgical treatment was amputation, which meant almost certain death. The only medicines were morphine, which was always scarce, and whiskey, which the surgeons and orderlies drank themselves. It is hard to blame them.

Not long after Shiloh, Eliza and her mother must have had to take to the woods. A band of freebooters, the Kansas Jayhawkers, rode into the county to burn houses and barns, shoot whatever was walking around, and collect any edibles the commissariat had missed. Fortunately, they made an early stop at the hospital, where they found a barrel of booze in the dispensary and got too drunk to ride. Next day, inexplicably, they went off. They were not the last to rampage through Oxford. General Grant and his army passed through; gray-coated and grizzled Nathan Bedford Forrest and his ragged troops came and went. By then the civilians were too hungry and terrified to care which side was which. There was nothing to eat, no medicine, and no news but death. In August, 1864, the U.S. Army came back to Oxford once more and burned it to the ground. The women gathered at the outskirts of the burning village and wept aloud in the roadway. Eliza, if she was among them, would have been eleven years old, with nothing to look back upon but hardship occasionally interrupted by chaos and insanity. Did she watch while any of the 700 graves were dug on the university campus? How did she construe the ways of her elders and her betters?

The war was over in April, 1865, but Appomattox cannot have seemed much of an event to Eliza. At least no more armies arrived and departed. Like the thousands of other children born in the South in the 1850s, she looked out upon a barren landscape. Nothing had any value — currency, bonds, land, all were equally valueless. The villages were gone, the countryside ravaged, the livestock slaughtered and eaten. There was no money for seed, and no credit at the store, and no store. The railroads, which once had carried fruit and vegetables to markets north of Lafayette County, were ruined. The men who managed to return from the war had come back mutilated or deathly ill. In family after family, the resourcefulness and strength of the women were the only hope of survival. And into this wasteland, too, came the newly liberated black men and women of northern Mississippi, free at last and more ragged even than Eliza's kind. For the first time the white and black laborers of the South would get a close look at one another and would learn to make do somehow as neighbors. Separate but equal, in the democracy of want.

I don't know how Eliza managed, but she and her family did not starve, nor did she die in the epidemics of yellow fever that had regularly carried off large sections of the population of northern Mississippi and now truly came with a vengeance after the war. She grew up and married a young man named Tillman McElroy. His older brother, Scott, was a veteran, one of the few who had come back with his arms and legs and eyesight intact; Tillman and Eliza settled down on a farm near his. One day in 1880, the census taker came and counted them, a fine young family with three children. He wrote down all their names and ages. He did not write down that the economic depression was unimproved since 1865 or that in one recent summer, 16,000 people had died in a local epidemic of yellow fever. For white as well as black an inevitable slide into serfdom had begun. During the two decades after the war, the poor whites, along with the blacks, whose emancipation turned out to be at best theoretical, were enslaved by landholders who had less regard for their victims than they had for chattel. A man's slaves, at least, were a fiscal responsibility, and even a moral one, but sharecroppers and tenant farmers were no one's responsibility. If they died, it was their own fault.

Some time in the 1880s the McElroys took flight, traveling in wagons as their forefathers had, leading their livestock by the bridle and their small children by the hand. They crossed the Mississippi River on a ferryboat to Helena, Arkansas, and went on into the wilderness. All the way from the back-country of North Carolina, all the way from Ulster. They came, eventually, to the Ouachita River Valley in central Arkansas and made a clearing for themselves and proceeded to build a village of their own. Visions of it wake my Aunt Laura in the middle of the night; sometimes she takes paper and pen and tries to describe these visions for me. There was a fine log house, she says, where Eliza gave birth to many children. There was a sawmill, a gristmill, a sorghum press. They cut their own lumber, raised corn and cotton. The smokehouse was always full of hams, and the cooling box at the springhouse brimmed over with butter and eggs and sweet milk. Nothing could touch this family now, no wars, no epidemics. They never needed to go to town. Having marched across half a continent, the old anarchists thought they had won their gamble at last and had built their own citadel, a self-sufficient unit that should have endured forever, even if the rest of humanity had disappeared overnight.

Now only Laura remembers Eliza or any of the women of that time. Eliza and Tillman are in a burying ground that only cemetery aficionados know how to find any more. They lie there under the same stone, shaded by cedar trees and dogwood. I love the cedar trees, particularly; they are like old women, thick in the middle, their branches as thin as old arms, and their scant foliage gray as hair. One recollection my mother had of Eliza McElroy was how she would sit outdoors to air her topknot: "She would bring a straight-legged chair out in the sunshine and let me take all the hairpins out and shake down the hair and comb it with a fine-toothed comb. That's how she kept it clean, you know. They hardly ever washed their hair in those days. They cleaned it with that fine-toothed comb in the sunshine, and they always wore their sunbonnets to keep the dust off. That's what the sunbonnets were for — not to keep the sun out of their eyes."

What delighted Eliza most was quilting: bending over a basket of scraps, scissoring up the little pieces, stitching them together with fine white thread (every stitch all but invisible, every one perfectly even) until she had four dozen wedding rings or log-cabin blocks or a hundred patchwork butterflies. When she got the whole opus on a frame, she would weave the needle through the quilt top, the batting, and the backing, making the same rapid, even stitches, in a line straight as the drop of a plumb bob. "Druther quilt than anything in the round world," she would say. So far as anybody knew, it was the one thing she did for the pure joy of it. She quilted even though she needed no more quilts.

She also had some quality that even Aunt Laura can scarcely describe. She was steady. She never got upset or lost her temper. Her dignity was absolute. Animals obeyed her. Children loved her. She would play games with them, dress their dolls, show them how to make turkey callers out of a piece of wood. Her sons and daughters, even as grown-ups, thought it a privilege to sit beside her at table. She said no more than was absolutely necessary and never spoke of the times when history in its senselessness and disorder had blundered across her doorstep. If she ended her days self-possessed and serene, she had won these qualities in a fair fight.

Tillman and Eliza have lain under their cedar trees half a century now; even their great-grandchildren are beginning to grow old. And except for a few jagged potsherds scattered close to the site (a set of blacksmithing tools, a wheelwright's awl, a scythe handle my Uncle Cecil keeps in an old shed as curiosities) the McElroy world is gone, inundated like the continent of Atlantis. Wealth dug out of the Southern earth is often turned back under it again, and the valley claimed and cleared by the McElroys — the village shimmering before Aunt Laura's eyes as she dozes and wakes uneasily on her bed — was years ago overtaken by a flood, swallowed up in one gulp.

Around 1950, the Arkansas Power and Light Company, aided by the Army Corps of Engineers and substantial federal funding, dammed up the Ouachita River, flooding large portions of three counties and creating the third and most

magnificent of the three lakes that lie in the environs of Hot
Springs. The dam had been planned for many years. Farm
after farm, all the hard-won acreage, was bought up gradually by the Company. They'll have to float us out, was what
my Uncle Cecil said. He and Frances stayed on with their
fellow creature the mule and raised a crop the year that
the water began to rise.

Some of the area residents could hardly bear to speak of
what was happening to them, dreading the day when all
the well-loved villages would go under. They examined
maps. Would they lose Buckville? Crystal Springs? Cedar
Glades? All the rich bottom land? Porter Brown's bottom,
as the best farm in the county was called — a little local
joke. Possum Kingdom? Bear? All to be flooded. Oh, no, it
couldn't be. But there were young men back home from the
Army who were sick of farming, men waiting in hope that
work on the dam would soon begin. Big federal projects, of
course, make good jobs, better than harvesting logs in the
woods and hoisting them onto rickety truck beds or than
standing over a screaming apparatus in the Mountain Pine
sawmill or raising corn on shares.

And at last the dam got under way, a giant earthworks
in the throat of the green river, a retaining wall creating
an immense basin for sunperch and bass, crappie, catfish,
water moccasins, turtles. The men who supplied the common labor on the dam, who handled the picks and shovels,
piled the rock in dump trucks and hauled it in, drove the
bulldozers, and poured the concrete, thereby earning the
first decent wages of their lives, were the impoverished sons
and grandsons of the first claimants of the land, black and
white together, toiling to obliterate their birthplace. Tillman and Eliza's grandsons were among them, and Lavisa's
sons. They were glad to get the money, unafraid of the work.
They could split rocks all day and never drop in their tracks
with heatstroke. Pour it on, boys, we can do it.

But before the sluice gates were closed, these same men
went from one old burying ground to another, prying up
the stones, disinterring the rotting coffins, and laying them

ceremoniously to rest on higher ground. They moved a few of the old farmhouses, schools, and churches. They saved what they could. The cemetery where my grandparents and great-grandparents lie did not have to be uprooted, but the churchhouse where they all had sat so many Sundays had to be picked up and put down a little farther up the hillside. The water rose right up to the edge of the burying ground, and now the worn stones stand by the shore of the lake, pine boxes under the cedar and hickory trees, the red clay mounded up over them and baked hard in the sun, with winter's minute rivulets faithfully preserved in the rough texture.

On Decoration Day, the second Sunday in June each year, there is a festival in this graveyard. The survivors and descendants come to weed the graves and sweep them clean, just as the front yards used to be weeded and swept around the houses that the dead once occupied. Since each mound is the exact length of the coffin beneath, it is clear which graves are children's, and many infant bodies have been laid here. We who come on Decoration Day read the names and dates and try to remember all that we can. On these mounds, as austere and primitive as any in the annals of anthropology, we firmly plant plastic nosegays. "I hate putting artificial flowers, Honey," explains my Aunt Emogene in her gentle way. She always was the family beauty, and her brick-brown hair is coiled high on her head as she sets a false chrysanthemum in the earth. "But you know, if we were to put real ones, they'd be gone by tomorrow in this hot sun. This way I can be sure there's always a flower here."

And so the polyethylene daisies and hot pink plastic roses tap stiffly against one another in the breeze, and the stark churchyard looks gay and well kempt. From time to time they have a burial here, but the cemetry is almost full now, and the progeny of those who lie in it will buy their funeral plots in some garden of perpetual care or go compactly to their rest in the form of ashes.

On this day, which also includes an all-day singing and

dinner on the ground, the old church is reopened. As a piece of architecture, it is as simple as a child's drawing, a white wooden box set high off the ground on bricks stacked at each corner. The windows run all the way around, and when these are propped open, a miraculous summer breeze cools the congregation. The upright piano is taken out of its crate, and my cousin Donna skillfully beats some gospel music out of the tuneless old pile, while a man in a yellow suit and string tie (a Grand Ole Opry dandy) plays a banjo. We all sit down on the unpainted pews that were nailed to the church floor almost a century ago, hard and discomfiting as a preacher's stare. There once was a fat iron stove in the middle of the floor, but now that the church is opened only for this one day in June, the stove has been taken away.

Shoes pat the floor, Donna hammers the piano faster, and up go the voices, singing sharp and flat and in all keys. "Just like a tree that's standing by the water, I shall not be moved." My two citified little daughters look at me in astonishment as I sing out. The music stops, and a very old man, his frame crumpled like a paper doll's, one eye askew, stands up and voices his thankfulness at having been spared by the Lord to come here another year. And then they read the long list, as they always do, of this year's dead, and from the congregation come a few extra names — "Aunt Hannah Robbins passed away in March." "You never mentioned poor old Mr. Beasley."

There are no other faces like these faces. They have the mark of the backwoods on them, and even the most youthful among them conform to no modern standard of beauty. The chins jut, the jowls hang, there are wens and warts and bald spots, stooped shoulders, short waists, huge square hands, freckles everywhere, pounds and pounds of fat that surely ought to be dieted off: there are no joggers around here. But their earnestness and good nature are almost palpable in the air, and the poverty that some of them have known shows so nakedly in their faces that I suddenly am unable to find voice enough to sing with them of the mansions Jesus is readying for us all in heaven. A number of those who sit in this church are as remote from its culture as I am: day trippers, brushing up our country manners, slapping too many backs, laughing too loudly, careful not to use our city grammar, and gratefully expecting to return soon to air conditioning and a Scotch and soda. But the rest of the people truly mean what they sing in the Heavenly Highway Hymn Book. "I care not for your earthly treasures." "Oh, how the love of Jesus lifted me."

Outdoors, a mammoth dinner is spread on card tables or simply on old quilts laid down on the sparse grass — all the good eats of a country picnic, the vats of fried chicken, the twenty varieties of cakes and quickbreads, the potato salad everybody hopes had not gone bad in the 95 degree heat. We all go around sampling things, fixing plates for the very young and the very old, urging them to eat, trying to get the toddlers to nap for an hour in the shade. We hug each others' sweaty necks and smack each others' cheeks. We grope perplexedly for names. "Why, you're Velma's daughter!" they exclaim. "Darlin', I knew your grandma well."

Over and over again I tell my maiden name and my mother's maiden name and Grandma's maiden name, and they relay the same information about themselves, in the obsessive and peculiarly Southern quest for common ancestry, the urgent hope of discovering mutual cousins by marriage. Someone presses upon me the name of a former resident of the area now living in Scarsdale, New York — in case I ever badly need to see homefolks and am unable to come all the way home at the moment. In the backwoods you learned to love your own and mistrust foreigners, but you tried if possible to make everybody your own, seeking kinship bonds with any and all comers, trying by whatever means to connect yourself with the rest of humanity, raking up ancestral names ("Now, Great-Aunt Addie was a Holloway"), uncovering the secret network of cousinship.

As the feast goes on, I become a feast for the chiggers and woodticks, which prefer urban flesh when any is to be had, and soon I am scratching frenziedly while I delineate my bloodlines and embrace my mother's half sister's grand-daughters. My legs pop out in tormenting red welts, the heat is overwhelming. Inside the church the banjo and the piano still play, and some impromptu gospel quartets have formed up, but I have to go off and sit down by myself in the shade. There are too many of my dead here, too many of them rising up and seating themselves on the benches in that harsh country church.

Beyond the graveyard, the lake is beautiful and wild, its thousand miles of shore line untouched by the real estate developments that often spring up in such places. It is one of the largest lakes in the South and is an important part of the local economy, attracting many campers and vaca-tioners. Parts of it are almost uncharted, and it is dotted with islands, once hilltops. Hunters sometimes get lost on these promontories for days at a time. Lacking a compass and sufficient provisions, a few of them have gotten per-manently lost. And there are places where the water is so deep and the lake bed so thick with stumps that if a fish-erman falls out of his boat and drowns, the sheriff does not bother to dredge for the body. I have heard of several be-reaved and luckless families who, lacking proof of death, have been unable to collect the life insurance.

But with a good boat and a reliable guide, you can easily navigate the old drowned communities. ("Here is where the school building was, here the mountain where we hunted deer, over that way was the old homeplace.") And you can imagine, swollen like bodies and bobbing along the surface of the bottomless mud below, the rail fences, the disman-tled houses and barns. You can peer into the depths looking for iron washpots, brass bedsteads, chimneys, garden gates, the stiles that marched over many a fence, the pine and oak and sweet gum skeletons, the massive, undulating roots of the oak in Lavisa's immaculate front yard where my cous-ins and I used to make a playhouse. You can imagine that you see women in the lake, our ancestresses, tall, strong women with muscles in their arms, their hair skinned back and tied up in a knot behind their heads like Indians, their feet in heavy shoes. With children at their skirt tails, the women hoe and plant. They bend over caldrons of steaming water and boiling oil. They turn legs of pork in the smokehouse. They set cranky old hens on a nest and beak the chicks, turn cream into sweet butter, spin raw cotton into fine thread. They chew tobacco and dip snuff. They go to church and sing out loud about Jesus. They are sorceresses. No one remembers their names.

Here at the bottom of the lake, forever lost unless some enterprising aquatic archaeologist recovers it in the distant future, lies the end of the Southern frontier and of headlong migration that began two centuries ago in the Carolina backwoods, a way of life forgotten, a definition of womanhood that might allay our fear and calm our anger, if we could remember what we used to be.

Four

The Servant Problem

"We're used to living around 'em. You Northerners aren't. You don't know anything about 'em." This is or was the all-purpose utterance of white Southerners about blacks. Everybody from Jefferson Davis to Strom Thurmond has said it, in some version, at one time or another. Turned on its obverse, the old saw means, "You can't know how bad they are." Or, conversely, "You can't imagine how deeply we understand them." This racial intimacy has served as the explanation of everything from lynch mobs to the recent and comparatively peaceful integration of Southern schools, accomplished while Boston and Detroit sometimes literally went up in flames.

I grew up hearing about this interracial coziness or reading about it in novels, and for years I believed in it. But in fact it simply did not exist, at least not for me. With one exception, the only people I ever knew were white. I had no little black buddy to go fishing with me under the railroad bridge in the summertime. My copious black nurse had no wide-eyed, pigtailed offspring hanging around the kitchen wanting to play jacks: I didn't have a black nurse.

No black children went to my school — to this day I have no idea where any black primary schools were even located.

Several thousand black people lived in Hot Springs, of course, in three or four different tumbledown sections that butted right up against equally tumbledown white neighborhoods. I always saw more black men than women. Black men ran the elevators in the three or four buildings where doctors and dentists had offices. They swept the floors and emptied the spittoons in the casino where my father worked. (I was not allowed inside a gambling house, even to visit my dad, but he used to tell me about the high rollers from New York who would tip the black porter twenty dollars.) Black men worked as garbage collectors, as waiters, as kitchen help — sometimes as yard men, though elderly white men most often claimed such jobs.

Besides the kitchen help and porters there existed, according to my father, an utterly terrifying class of Negroes who got drunk and went after each other with razors on Saturday nights. Their names and crimes would be listed in the newspapers in the "Colored" column on Mondays. Some of these razor artists, Daddy said, were also burglars and did even more dreadful things, such as attacking white women. For this, in his opinion, no punishment could quite suffice. Luckily, he said, it didn't happen too often.

I never saw hide or hair of these bad men with their razors, but I knew a few of the well-behaved black men by name. For example, I knew Crip, who ran the elevator in the Medical Arts Building, a twelve-story skyscraper where all the dentists had offices. My teeth rotted continuously, so Mother and I got quite familiar with Crip, white-haired, bent forward at the middle, his joints twisted by arthritis into grotesque knots of agony. He always put on the most astonishing act. My father's nickname in the gambling world was Hat, as Crip knew, since his son worked as a casino porter, so Crip called my mother Miz Hat. "Why, mornin', Miz Hat," and he would hand her in and out of the creaky old elevator cage as though she were some plantation queen mounting and dismounting her blooded steed. I was Little Miz Hat, and he would bow and scrape and somehow make me feverishly aware of my adorable blonde curls. In the elevator was a little jump seat for the operator, but he never would sit down in the presence of whites and would set me on the jump seat instead. I don't know how my mother felt about all this, but I loved it. It made me feel that my mother and I were ladies. Why else would this poor old man act so silly?

Black women were a complete mystery to me. In those days, surely, most black women earned their livings as domestics, and yet I knew scarcely any family who kept a maid. Even washerwomen or women who took in ironing were usually white. When I was about seven, my father got a raise and decided to hire a maid for my mother — over her objections, for she was quite capable of keeping the house clean by herself and would rather have banked the money. But Daddy wanted his wife to have some leisure, and so one morning, very early, he brought Emma to our back door. For the two or three years that we were able to afford her, he would go and fetch her in the car six mornings a week, and then Mother would drive her home again in the afternoon. Emma earned ten dollars a week and Daddy, sixty-five (he too worked six days out of seven). He forbade me to tell any of the neighbor children what Emma's salary was, since the going rate was a dollar a day and sometimes less. But Mother had said she would be ashamed to work anybody for a dollar a day, and Daddy was eager to pay ten dollars, and bonuses.

Thus commenced my only childhood association with a black woman. Emma was five feet tall, round but not fat, and so black that her facial features, quite delicate and small, seemed indistinct. Her eyes were blacker than her skin and seemed to have no whites to them. Though she looked like a girl, she was already a grandmother. Watching her as she expertly thrust the point of the iron into ruffles and pleats, I used to beg to touch the palms of her hands, which were the color of cream slipper satin, and when I asked her how she got her palms so light, she would laugh and say it was from washing on a rub-board.

I was already corrupted, perhaps by books, perhaps by Emma's shy deference toward me. I wanted to play the daughter of the manor. How wonderful to have a maid to order around. Now, I thought, Mother could take me swimming on summer afternoons, or we could go to the movies every day. I could leave wet towels on the bathroom floor and scatter dirty socks around my bedroom and change clothes three times a day. But Mother quickly set me straight again. The first time she heard me bragging to the neighborhood children that we had a maid, she gave me a switching. She grew tougher than ever on the issue of picking up dirty socks and being careful with fresh-ironed dresses. And one morning, when Emma told me to drink my milk, and I told her not to boss me around, Mother came in and whipped me with the fly swatter — a favorite tool. (The rubber ones were far worse than the wire screen kind.) According to Mother, Emma was there to tell me what to do, not the reverse. And worse than that, my dream of becoming a pampered child of the leisure classes vanished as Mother proceeded to work side by side with Emma.

Together on a Monday morning they would set the white linens boiling on the stove and then heft the caldron to the washing machine on the back porch: it was an "automatic" that had to be filled and emptied by hose. Together they fished the steaming sheets out of the soapsuds and fed them through the wringer. Two black arms and two sunburnt freckled ones pumped up and down in the rinse tubs. Mother and Emma hung everything on the line just so, right side out and hems down. Before the days of Emma, lunch on washdays had been a piece of bread, and supper, bacon and eggs — the wages of exhaustion. But now the laundry was finished at noon, and by three o'clock the clean, sweet fragrance of fresh-ironed cotton pervaded the house. While one of the women ironed, the other would peel the vegetables for the pot roast and cut up a salad, maybe even stir up a cake or pudding.

Instead of saving labor for my mother, having a house-maid simply empowered her to do more work: to bake pies on washdays and iron the clothes more fanatically, to wax the floors twice as often and "do up" the curtains four times a year instead of once. For me, yearning for a life of indolence and pleasure, which I would spend rambling around in dime stores with my mother, it only meant that while I played paper dolls or dressed the dog in baby bonnets, two women were working in the kitchen instead of just one. On school days it meant that I arrived in a house where all the chores had been so meticulously done that I could fling myself down beside the radio and soak up Tom Mix, the Lone Ranger, and the Shadow.

The whole arrangement drove my father crazy. On the one hand, he would beg, command, my mother to get dressed at least one afternoon a week and leave the house to Emma. They had regular, angry arguments about it, with my mother saying grimly, "Hat, I'm not fixing to do that. Why don't you leave me alone?" And he would keep on until she began to cry, and then he would upbraid her for crying. On the other hand, Emma drove him crazy. He couldn't understand why she wouldn't sit at the supper table with us. It offended his working-class sympathies to see her sitting on a stool at the Hoosier cabinet or waiting stubbornly until we three had left the table. Nor could he quite understand why she refused to come and go by the front door.

I don't claim that my mother's way of managing her black maid was typical. Most white women did not help their laundresses hang the washing on the line. Nor do I have any idea what Emma really thought of this hard-driving farm woman who insisted on equality in a basically unequal situation. Nor, even yet, do I wholly understand why my mother did what she did. Compulsive housewifery had some part in it. So did her upbringing. If she wanted Emma to be her sister rather than her servant, it was because the work made them sisters, and because out on the farm nobody but a parasite or an invalid or a baby sat still while other people worked.

There was another motive, too. As I went my way in this small Southern town, I began gradually to perceive that in the relationship between white women and black people lay an ominous political assumption that cut in two directions. Had she used Emma in just the right way, Mother could have become a lady. But Mother didn't want to be a lady. Something in her was against it, and she couldn't explain what frightened her, which was why she cried when my father ridiculed her. Siding with my father, as I invariably did at that epoch, I thought Mother was foolish and countrified. A bumpkin. Why would anybody refuse to be a lady? I sure intended to be a lady when I grew up. But Mother's aversion stuck with me somehow and had its effect.

* * *

Small girls these days don't worry anymore, I hope, about whether to grow up and be ladies, but the question tormented me, even before I understood the political implications. That the daughter of a bookmaker and a farm woman in the middle of Arkansas in the 1940s should fret about such a thing is illogical if not ludicrous — but the obsession came quite naturally. At about the age of eight or nine, I had turned into a terminally addicted bookworm, and the book I loved most was *Gone With the Wind*. I read it all the time. I used to layer an Oz book or the Andersen fairy tales or Nancy Drew between long stretches of Margaret Mitchell, and later on I salted Scarlett and Rhett with Louisa May Alcott, Charlotte Brontë, Dickens, Frank Yerby, Samuel Shellabarger, thousands or perhaps millions of comic books, and everything else that came my way, particularly historical novels with heavy breathing. But I never gave up *Gone With the Wind*. I still read it.

What draws me, besides the drive of the plot, is the power and clarity of the female characters. The women in the book

function as the electrical charge that holds the South together. All the men are flawed — Gerald O'Hara is a baby,
Ashley Wilkes passive and helpless, and Rhett Butler, for
all his elegant machismo, is cold and mean and sarcastic.
The women fight the battles and get along a lot better than
the men. Not just Scarlett or the saintly Melanie, who both
grow predictable and cloying to even the most devoted
reader. But the minor characters — Beatrice Tarleton with
fiery red hair and eight children, who wears, not hoopskirts, but a riding habit and understands horses better than
any man in the county. Dolly Merriwether, the dowager
queen of Atlanta, and Grandma Fontaine, the bony old lady
who has lived through the Indian wars of an earlier generation and who claims that her ancestors have been run out
of three European countries and the island of Haiti as well
before getting licked by the Yankees. "But we always turn
up on top in a few years," she says. And there are a dozen
others, too, vivid and tough. Nowhere before in American
fiction had there been women of this caliber. Plucky heroines, maybe. Brave or independent. Strong-minded, like Jo
March. But not tough.

I always took these women literally, as portraits of real
people the author had known personally or had heard stories about in the Georgia uplands. Margaret Mitchell, as
everyone knows, worked ten years on her one masterwork
and so far as I know, has never been caught in the smallest
technical inaccuracy. The book may or may not be stuffed
with truth, but it is stuffed with facts — information about
food, fabric, furnishings (if she says that Scarlett carried a
cambric handkerchief, you can be sure that's what ladies'
handkerchiefs were made of in those days). What I did not
realize was that the author had read a lot of historical novels, too, and that some of her characters came not from life
but from books. That is, they were sterotypes.

One of the most important of the women characters falls
into that category: Ellen O'Hara is the archetype of the
Southern lady, an authoritative definition of the species, and
the first honest-to-God Southern lady I had ever met, in or

out of a book. Ellen simply enraptured me. What luck for those three O'Hara girls to have such a silky darling for a mother! I did not know, nor would I have cared, that plantation mistresses like Ellen had been stock characters on the literary landscape for a hundred years already. Plantation novels had periodically been best sellers in America since an opus called *Swallow Barn* came out in 1832.

Ellen is the highborn wife of Gerald O'Hara, an Irishman on the make who won his Georgia plantation in a card game. Then he caught Ellen, a Savannah beauty suffering from a misbegotten attachment to a rakehell cousin who was killed in a brawl. Ellen never loves Gerald, but she represses her grief and walks the earth in a halo of piety and wifely loyalty. Practical and ethereal all at once, she is the mainstay of Tara's economy, which she regulates with the combined powers of queen and prime minister. Naturally, she contrives to cover up her executive abilities so as not to embarrass her husband or startle the servants. But whether she is supervising the poultry yard or merely suppressing her true feelings, her forte is management.

But Ellen's essential role is not vis-à-vis Gerald or even their three daughters. It is her nurture of the slaves at Tara, who work all day in the field or the great house but are helpless as babies when night comes and they have an opportunity to live their own lives. Georgia slaves, if they were anything like Ellen's, must have been very odd people. They apparently had no sex lives. Only one black baby is born in the whole novel; only two of the Tara house servants, Dilcey and Pork, are married. When Prissy says that she "doan know nothin' 'bout birthin' babies," she is apparently speaking for all her kind. The only black women with a grain of sense at Tara are the two ponderous housemaids, Mammy and Dilcey. However, instead of sending them down to the quarters to oversee life's crucial events, Ellen herself makes house calls.

Nighttime finds her down at the cabins ministering, presiding over sickbeds and deathbeds. When the novel opens, she has just returned, however, from charity work further

up the social ladder — midwifing the birth of an illegitimate white baby — for the white trash make as many demands on Ellen as the slaves. But wherever her nightly ex-
ertions may have taken her, Ellen is always at breakfast the
next morning, catering to her husband's notions and settling her daughters' spats. When the great news from Fort
Sumter alters the course of her life, Ellen never pauses to
wonder what kind of folly the gentlemen might be up to.
She simply swings into action to maximize production at
Tara. She meets her quotas for the Confederate commissariat and rolls her bandages. Before the war is over, Ellen
catches typhoid and dies — graciously saving Tara as she
lies ill because General Sherman's lieutenant refuses to burn
a mansion with a lady in it.

This is the Southern lady at her height — not a woman
but a mode — "the magnolia grandiflora of a race of Cavaliers," as a piece of 1920s rhetoric had it. She is a goddess,
an immaculate angel hovering over the hearthside and the
slave shanty, floating in clouds of crinoline and silk, Virgin
and Mother, an altogether amazing creation. She is omni-
potent and subordinate, reticent and wise — qualities that
certainly link her to all other ladies on all other pedestals
and relate her to the mid-nineteenth-century ideal of upper
echelon womanhood.

Of course ladies existed in other times and places — not
only in the American South. French ladies, English ladies,
and Yankee ladies might (in theory at least) be equally
ethereal and reticent and loyal, but they were also supposed to be idle, delicate, slightly neurotic, and ill. Southern ladies, by way of contrast, had to work. Whether they
actually did or not varied from place to place, but the theory was that they worked — not because they lacked servants but precisely because they did not. In fact, the richer
the lady, the greater the job. Any lady who qualified as such
had to have a few slaves. Very rich ladies might have ten
or twenty or even more. Dozens more, perhaps, than even
the grandest English country mansion would have required. Managing servants has always been a headache for

the wealthy matron, but in the South it was not only the occasionally inflated numbers of servants in a given household but their wholly dependent status that made the responsibility loom so large. Who was going to look after all these souls if not the Southern lady?

In 1897, thirty-five years before Ellen O'Hara was set down on paper, a Virginia literary man wrote a kind of idyll about the Southern goddess and her duties in life. Thomas Nelson Page was one of the best-known writers of his day. He specialized in dialect stories about good darkies ("O massa," his people went around saying, "de ole times was the bestis times ole Sam evah seed"). He also was an eloquent defender of the white man's right to lynch. (Page was by no means some regional joke. He served for many years as Woodrow Wilson's ambassador to Italy, and the President, who was a Virginian himself, referred to him as a "national ornament.") Like Margaret Mitchell, Page wrote at a moment of crippling economic depression in the South and the rest of the nation, when the children of the Confederacy were in a mood to look back bitterly on the world they had lost. Here, according to Page, is Dixie's queen mother:

> The plantation mistress was the most important personage about the home, the presence which pervaded the mansion, the centre of all that life, the queen of that realm; the master willingly and proudly yielding her entire management of all household matters and simply carrying out all her directions. . . . It would no more have occurred to him to make a suggestion about the management of the house than about that of one of his neighbors; simply because he knew her and acknowledged her infallibility. She was indeed a surprising creature — often delicate in frame and of a nervous organization so sensitive as to be a great sufferer; but her force and character pervaded and directed everything, as unseen yet as unmistakable as the power of gravity controls the particles that constitute the earth. She was . . . the keystone of the domestic economy which bound all the rest of the structure and gave it its strength and beauty. From early morn till morn again, the most important and delicate concerns of the plantation were in her charge and care . . . she was mistress,

manager, doctor, nurse, counsellor, seamstress, teacher, house-keeper, slave, all at once. . . . Her life was one long act of devotion to God, devotion to her husband, devotion to her children, devotion to her servants, to her friends, to the poor, to humanity. . . . She managed her family, regulated her servants, fed the poor, nursed the sick, consoled the bereaved. Who knew of the visits she paid to the cabins of her sick and suffering servants?

It is Ellen O'Hara, of course. Generations of orators have invoked her beauty before generations of state legislators. Her purity has been preached from the pulpits. Her luminous presence has stayed the very hand of death, and certainly the hand of the radical. When such a person needed protection, who could condone free blacks voting in elections? As a corrective to the reforms brought briefly about by Reconstruction — particularly black male suffrage — the Southern lady was better even than the fiery cross. She served as the pretext for any kind of violence the Ku Klux Klan could dream up. For as even Thomas Nelson Page must have seen, the Southern lady is not so much a real person as a utilitarian device for covering up ugly reality.

What makes her powerful is not her own perfection but her ability to mask the imperfections of the world. If the dragons of the Ku Klux Klan wanted to ride around in sheets terrifying defenseless people, what better rationale could they have than the need to protect *her*, and the blessed assurance that she would forgive them when they got home. White men have feared the sexuality of black men since the first slave ship put in at Jamestown, and, of course, they would imagine black hands being laid upon the person of the white goddess. But instead it would be Her hand, slim and cool, that would be laid on the sweaty brow of slavery. The lady's work was cut out for her, not in her own house or even in the quarters, but in the realm of collective self-delusion.

As long as she keeps to her plantation, the lady is the most satisfactory of all social creatures — an uncomplaining, unquestioning collaborator. She did not devise the system she serves so capably: to another will go all the credit, all the blame. She merely carries out her orders and ensures that things go smoothly. One of the strangest effects of the slave system upon slaveholders was that it demanded this kind of performance from several generations of white women, and the act proved to be so entertaining that it kept on running long after slavery was gone. The only catch is that the lady was in part hallucinatory. Sometimes she did not act like Ellen O'Hara at all. What Ellen O'Hara's origins were and what her real-life counterparts were like make an odd chapter in the annals of Southern womanhood.

* * *

Political image-making, which we sometimes think was perfected along with the cathode tube, is no novelty in the South. If the production of self-serving folklore qualified as an industry, the South would have been an industrial power since colonial times. The first heroes to emerge were the Tidewater aristocrats. These most distinguished of all immigrants to our shores were described, if not actually invented, by a mid-nineteenth-century lawyer and scribbler from Alabama named Daniel Hundley. They were, he said, "English courtiers of aristocratic mien and faultless manner . . . French Huguenots and Scotch Jacobites, the retainers and associates of Lord Baltimore . . . Spanish dons and French Catholics, a race of heroes and patriots." Hundley's *Social Relations in Our Southern States*, which appeared in 1860 as prewar propaganda went into full swing, was a sort of dictionary of received wisdom. His key figure was the cavalier. Whether Hundley had ever seen any cavaliers or not, he and his contemporaries firmly believed that somewhere, if not in the immediate vicinity, had lived a band of Southern noblemen who divided their time between riding their acres and reading philosophy in the well-stocked libraries of their stately homes.

Before the Revolutionary War, there were a few great families in the coastal South — Virginia's celebrated Randolphs, Carters, and Byrds, who lived more or less like English gentry and even had books in the house. And yet, a generation of scholars has proved that virtually no English or French aristocrats settled in the Southern colonies. The overwhelming majority of immigrants to Virginia and Maryland and South Carolina in colonial times were poor people. Half of them were actually indentured servants and convicts — not all of whom, contrary to rumor, went out and became the forefathers of hillbillies. The real American aristocrats, when there were any, built their fortunes after they got here, and they had little time for the pursuits and trappings of high culture.

As one pre-Revolutionary traveler observed in 1762, "The prudent management of a large Virginia Estate requires so frequent and so close an Inspection . . . that the Possessor . . . can expect but little of that Leisure and Repose, which are requisite for a pleasurable or successful Engagement in such Parts of Literature, as the Languages, Criticism, and Curious and Deep Researches into Antiquity." In a newly settled land, even the rich people worked. Charming and hospitable and genteel they may or may not have been, but they were not the aristocracy of Europe transplanted — no matter what their latter-day descendants wanted to believe.

Even if they had been, the old Tidewater culture based on rice, tobacco, and indigo was largely bankrupt and stagnant by the end of the eighteenth century. Had it not been for one simple invention, the Cavalier myth would certainly have died, and the Southern lady would never even have been heard of. But in 1793 a Massachusetts Yankee named Eli Whitney, who happened to be visiting friends on a Georgia farm, devised the cotton gin, and patented it the next year. It revolutionized the economy of the South, or at least set it going full tilt. Suddenly cotton was transformed from time-consuming nuisance to a highly profitable crop. It provided a whole new rationale for slavery, for cotton required almost year round labor. The market for it already existed in the mills of England. As the gin made cotton profitable, cotton made slavery profitable. A farmer could double his output with one good field hand. Thus a new class of planters, or immigrants hoping to become planters, began to push into the western South and up the Mississippi River in the early nineteenth century.

The cotton boom began just about the time that the Atlantic slave trade was closed by Act of Congress, in 1808. And the same decade saw the start of a population explosion that was to shake the Southern earth and have a profound effect on the lives of Southern women. In 1790, the slave population of the South had stood at 658,000. In 1810 it was over one million. By 1860 it was just under four million: in fifty years the slave force had quadrupled. In an attempt to explain this phenomenal upsurge, some historians have contended that the slave brokers were illegally importing hundreds of thousands of Africans. Others have claimed that the owners were practicing systematic mass breeding to compensate for the closing of the trade. But the historians who have looked at the evidence most recently find that neither of these explanations will hold.

Statistics on illegal imports hardly exist — smugglers being disinclined to keep records — but why import what can so readily and cheaply be raised at home? As to systematic breeding, Nazi style, it was undoubtedly beyond the cunning of most owners. In any case the black family, if not shattered on the auction block, was as strong and enduring and fertile a unit as any other kind of family. In his massive recent study *The Black Family in Slavery and Freedom*, Herbert Gutman observes that most owners set a high premium on slave women who bore many children, and thus — either for moral or for practical reasons — these men encouraged their slaves to marry and live in orderly family groupings. The soaring birthrate of both blacks and whites in the nineteenth century makes the whole South look like a breeding farm. From plantation to mountain top it was, in fact, a booming frontier. There was plenty to eat, lots of protein on the hoof, and more work to be done than there were people to do it. Babies were profitable, white ones, black ones. For the gentleman planter as for the dirt farmer, children were an important crop. They were wealth, or the source of it. And even for parents in bondage, children were a source of comfort, pleasure, purposefulness, joy.

The number of Southern slave owners was always proportionately small. At any given moment, there were more people who did not own slaves. In 1790, the 658,000 Southern slaves were held by about 79,000 families (only 23 per cent of all Southern families, the rest being slaveless). By 1850, over three million slaves were held by about 350,000 owners, and the average number of slaves per owner had increased from about eight to almost ten. The idea that the typical Southern planter owned hundreds of men and women, housed in row after row of shanties while he and his family lived in a shining mansion atop a hill, is simply a dream. In 1850 only two men owned as many as a thousand slaves; only nine owned as many as 500. The typical holding was five slaves; of the 350,000 owners, 310,000 had fewer than twenty.

What this meant for the slaves might vary from house to house, but what it meant for white Southern women was that in every generation, greater numbers of them found themselves in managerial roles with black servants. With fifty slaves on a rice plantation in South Carolina in 1780, a man would hire an overseer. With ten slaves on a cotton farm in Alabama in 1830, the man's wife would be the overseer. When women find themselves working at new jobs, whether running a brokerage firm, assembling machine guns, or supervising a cotton plantation, they have to devise a persona. How were they to behave? Where did their authority begin and end?

Willing or not, thousands of Southern women in the first half of the nineteenth century were confronted with this scenario. Ladies were no longer a luxury of upper-class life in the Tidewater. They were a managerial necessity, and a psychological and moral one as well. For if slavery was to be the foundation of economic life, and if one important crop on any large farm includes healthy black babies, a plantation becomes a complex domestic mechanism that can hardly be expected to function without a white woman around to figure out the endless details. Not only that, without her supposedly softening and mitigating influence around the place — or her mere cosmetic value — the whole operation quickly turns too rotten for a Christian to contemplate.

Right up until the Civil War, long after it as well, most Americans of any section would have agreed that blacks were an inferior race. In the accounts that white people give, the blacks vacillate between childishness and ferocity. They are children in need of food and clothing and the knowledge of God, but they are also savages. As late as 1930, two leading Southern intellectuals of the day were publicly vouching for just these same arguments. In the famous agrarian manifesto *I'll Take My Stand*, Robert Penn Warren argued against racial integration on the grounds that blacks were gentle, untrained children (later he utterly repudiated this view), while a few pages on, the historian Frank Owsley characterized the race as barely rehabilitated cannibals who had recently been cooking and eating one another in the Congolese rain forests.

But in 1930 as in 1830, no matter how much "evidence" there was that blacks were at once little children and man-eating barbarians, it was still hard to defend the basic propositions of chattel slavery. In a Christian, democratic nation, how can one human being own another? And if a man owns another, will he not sell that property against its will or abuse it or starve it? And if the property is female, what is to keep the owner from sexually exploiting it?

Not everybody worried about these ugly questions, but thoughtful people in the North and the South had a bad conscience about what the nation was permitting. Even if you accepted the idea that the slave was a savage in need of redemption, did that justify owning him? The first answer to be devised by the Southern apologists was that the self-interest of the owner would make him merciful. After all, only a fool would spend fifteen hundred dollars for a worker and then starve him to death. But it is hardly a watertight case. Men sometimes are fools. They lose their tempers and their reason, get drunk, beat their horses and their wives. Some are killers. The best of them make mistakes, overfarm their land, go broke. Where do the sunny principles of Adam Smith apply on a plantation, where it might be in somebody's interests to increase output even if it meant killing a few laborers?

As for the slave woman, she was doubly vulnerable in the system not only in her person but through her children. Even Thomas Jefferson, who himself appears to have had a long-term alliance with a slave woman, looked upon black children as a source of ready money. In 1819 Jefferson wrote a letter to his manager, who had carelessly allowed "5 little ones" to die. This was poor policy, Jefferson reminded the man, because " a child raised every 2 years is of more profit than the crop of the best laboring man. In this as in all other cases, Providence has made our interests and our duties coincide perfectly. . . ." Jefferson was hardly the last American to square up Providence and profit, but the same equation made other citizens uncomfortable.

There were other answers — better answers even than self-interest, which clearly was not going to go very far toward solving the moral problem. One possible riposte was that slavery was merely part of a universal scheme, the proper reflection, here below, of the divine order of things. God the Father ruled the universe, delegating some powers to man, who ruled the world as well as the women, children, and slaves who depended on him. Duty flowed upward on this ladder; authority and responsibility, downward. How else had society ever been held together? Each person had his proper and ordained place on earth as in heaven, and would be rewarded, as his superiors saw fit, for services rendered. And if this still were not enough to quiet the abolitionist whispers of the Christian conscience, then there was still an ace in the hole. That was the Southern lady.

In theory, anyhow, the lady would naturally stand between the victim and his tormentor. She would be the civilizing force. If the master tried to whip his slave, the lady would naturally stay his hand. If he tried to sell a black man away from his black wife, the lady would of course intercede with her lord. (Could he refuse her?) She would apportion the food and give extra rations to the sick. She would see that black bodies were clothed and black souls saved. And if the master showed any desire to seduce the housemaid, the very sight of the beautiful and virtuous woman who carried the keys to his household and mothered his fine white sons would certainly cause him to change his mind. The lady, in short, would function as the mother of the black race.

When Harriet Beecher Stowe set out to deliver the most killing blow she could muster against the Southern apologia for slavery (she was not a very perceptive critic of slavery itself, and she knew nothing about slaves), she loaded the dice as follows: She created a black man named Tom, a pious, de-sexed old toady if ever there was one. (According to one theory Tom is not a black man at all but the caricature in blackface of a properly submissive white wife.) She takes Tom out of his old Kentucky home and transports him, step by step, to a hellish place in Louisiana. The reason it is hellish is that it has no Southern lady. Simon Legree is not married. He is a vile old man with no idea how to run a home. In the end he beats poor Tom to death. If Legree had had a proper Southern lady for a wife, Mrs. Stowe could never have made things turn out that way. Mrs. Legree would have cleaned up the mess and made some curtains. She would have read the Bible before every meal, and if Legree had tried to beat anybody to death, she would have joshed him out of the notion. Harriet Beecher Stowe may not have known much about black men, but she obviously knew what Southern ladies were put on earth for. No lady, no apologia. It was as simple as that.

* * *

If there is any question, from the slaves' point of view, whether the Southern lady actually did mitigate their bondage, the answer, not surprisingly, is no. The flesh and blood Southern ladies did not measure up to their heavenly image. Of course white women lived on most plantations and farms and did their share of the work. A number of them must have been intelligent, capable, and tender-hearted. Many took on the role of family doctor for both white and black. But ministering angels? Looking at what few scraps remain of slaves' testimonials, I conclude that angels were as scarce then as now.

In the past decade or so, a new school of historians has come to the subject of slavery, and one of their methods is to use all kinds of heretofore untouched documentary evidence, particularly accounts that slaves, or freed slaves, have given of their experiences. Technically it was illegal to permit a slave to become literate, but even in those circumstances, a surprising number of such accounts — some of them speeches and interviews — have survived, and many have recently been published. I cannot claim to have read them all, but so far I have not come across so much as one reference to a white angel in female form. Once in a while a slave does speak of his mistress as a good woman, a merciful woman, a Christian. But if I had to characterize white mistresses from the memoirs I have read, I should have to say that as a group they were demanding, harsh, impatient, capricious, and quick to call for the laying on of the lash. Some were even sadists, with no redeeming qualities whatever.

Roving through a massive recent collection called *Slave Testimony: Two Centuries of Letters, Speeches, Interviews, and Autobiographies* edited by John W. Blassingame, I uncovered a few white ladies:

"What did ole missus look like? Well, I tell yer, honey, she looked like a witch. She'd set dere an' dat look 'ud come unto her eyes an' she'd study and study what to whip me about."

"While I worked in the house and waited upon my mistress, she always treated me kindly, but to other slaves, who were as faithful as I was, she was very cruel." The speaker, an ex-slave named James Curry, then describes how this woman once beat a black child to death.

"There was a woman slave who persisted in running away. Whippings did not frighten her, and so her mistress had her belled. An iron hoop was welded across her waist, another about her neck and attached to these a long rod went up her back to which, up over her head and beyond her reach, a bell was hung. It rang as she moved, and when she lay down at night the least motion started the clapper."

Women capable of torturing their servants may, one hopes, have been rare; yet they existed. (If Mrs. Stowe had been writing realistic fiction instead of an allegory, she could easily have had a Mrs. Legree more ferocious than Simon.) The records are full of other kinds of cruelty, too. Seven-day work weeks, maidservants required to sleep on the floor every night at the foot of their mistress's bed, slaves deprived of sleep and decent food or sent out to die in their old age — all this the work of white ladies. And running like a fine seam through the slave testimonials is the contempt of the servant for the mistress. What else could any reasonably intelligent able-bodied person have felt for a woman who might refuse to care for her own babies or mend her own clothing or even get out of bed in the middle of the night to fetch a glass of water for herself? Mistresses have always looked like fools to their servants. It has nothing necessarily to do with race.

Yet besides the sadists and tyrants and monsters of indolence, there were great numbers of white women who lived in harmony with their servants, women who did the best they could to remain human, even as the slaves remained human under adverse circumstances. In 1970, Anne Firor Scott, professor of history at Duke University, published *The Southern Lady*, which has become a classic among students of women's history. Anne Scott was the first to perceive that the notion of "lady" in the South was an invention of a slaveholding society, which, far from pampering its upper-class white women, demanded a great deal from them. Under slavery, of course, it was not only the slaves who must know their place and keep it, but everybody. The role played by the women of the ruling class is critical, for it is up to them to enforce the system. If they don't believe in it, or if the mistress of a plantation has no respect for the master, what then?

Thus it was that every possible argument — theological, philosophical, sexual, and economic — was martialed to convince these women that they were by nature subordinated to men and that they must fulfill their proper roles. George Fitzhugh, a proslavery philosopher of the antebellum South and a defender of the patriarchal society, knew very well that women were the key — for if they refused to stay put in the hierarchy, society would collapse. Fitzhugh, understandably, was in favor of early indoctrination, and so were most other Southern males. As Anne Scott writes, "Churches, schools, parents, books, magazines, all promulgated the same message: Be a lady and you will be loved and respected and supported." A woman's job was to marry early, please her husband in all ways, be a model of Christian piety, and as the kindly overseer of the slaves and the children, carefully train the young of both races to play the roles expected of them and thus to perpetuate the social system indefinitely. Most of these upper-class women, who might have started a civil war on their own had they known how, tried instead, as Professor Scott writes, "to live up to the Sisyphean task expected of them."

But this hardly resulted in a race of Ellen O'Haras. How different was the reality from the dream. First of all, the work that these women were expected to perform was overwhelming, and the diaries of new brides are full of complaints about the managerial duties thrust on them, usually on the very same day they entered their new homes as teen-aged brides. Not only might there be scores of servants to supervise, there was also the endless work of large farms or plantations or main houses to organize and get done.

Within a year, most of the new wives would be new mothers. Like their sisters on the frontier or in the slave quarters, the ladies bore as many babies as they were physically able to bear — eleven, twelve, fifteen. Today, even in the vast population of a city like New York, pregnancy is still unusual enough to be noticed. Most women one sees are not pregnant. On a large antebellum plantation, most women must have been pregnant most of the time from their late teens onward. The most striking feature of the human landscape in the Old South must not have been hoopskirts and parasols but round bellies. Those presumably reticent Southern ladies, who hated to spoil their fine figures and felt so shamed by being with child that they scarcely had a name for the condition, might spend twenty-five years (out of a lifespan of perhaps fifty) pregnant or recovering from childbirth or expecting momentarily to become pregnant again. Moreover, it was not only their figures that they risked losing. The result of pregnancy was very often death.

As to what these women thought of their slaves and how they treated them, it is hard to generalize. In the memoirs and diaries that they occasionally left, Southern ladies often speak of their servants as "children." One wonders whether, if they "mothered" these children, it was not mothering in the negative sense of that word — nagging, interfering, scolding.

Many of the wealthy women of the South felt their responsibilities deeply and expected to answer to God for every black soul in their households. However, except in novels, selflessness does not seem to have been any more stylish in 1855 than in 1980. One testimony from the mistress of black servants comes from a Georgia woman named Margaret Ward. In the 1880s she appeared before a Senate committee that was touring the nation to investigate the condition of "capital and labor." "I do think," declared Mrs. Ward to the committee chairman, "that if a Southern woman ever arrives at the Celestial City she ought to go very high up." Mrs. Ward was forty-two when she testified and the wife of a prosperous merchant in Birmingham, Alabama. Before the war, she had lived in Rome, Georgia. She was delighted to go into detail about her life in the old days. Her attitude toward her servants was completely tough-minded. Her homeplace in Rome was hardly the kindergarten Tara was.

Mrs. Ward recalled: "I do not suppose we ever had less than three servants who were very good cooks, and it generally took three to do the cooking . . . then we had our regular washerwomen. In those days we would always have in one of the cabins close by the house one or two washerwomen, who took the clothes out on Monday morning and washed them straight through the week, never being in a hurry because they had nothing else to do. Then there were house girls around ad libitum, three or four at least in every house that were being raised up and trained as servants . . . they were really splendid house servants . . . then seamstresses were regular institutions in the house in those days."

All these workers needed supervision, of course. "A Southern lady's life before the war was by no means an idle one." By the 1880s, however, the servant problem had gotten worse, as the servant problem always does. "It is a very hard life that we housekeepers here lead . . . they [the maids] are as careless as they can be about everything, and altogether, they are very trying." When the senator from New Hampshire responded with the suggestion that she hire white servants, Mrs. Ward cried, "Oh mercy! I wouldn't give them room. We would all go distracted if we had them for servants. Their only idea of doing work for us is to do it as they do it for themselves, which is no way at all. . . . It is like home to have the colored ones around us, even though they are trifling." The senators' interest in the laboring classes did not carry them so far as to interview Mrs. Ward's household help. But surely these workers did not perceive their boss as a ministering angel.

Collaborators though they may have been in the institution of slavery, Southern women often turn up as closet abolitionists. "I hate slavery," wrote the most famous of all Southern diarists, Mary Chesnut. "All Southern women are abolitionists at heart." Some women hated the system, some hated the slaves, and some both. Others saw well enough what the crimes of slavery were. Ellen Glasgow, the Virginia novelist, wrote of hearing her mother say, many years after the Civil War was over, "Even in the midst of the horrors a wave of thankfulness rushed over me when I heard that the slaves were freed." And through the hundred or more diaries published by Southern women after the war runs the same leitmotif. They hated Yankees, but they had hated slavery, too — Judith McGuire, Frances Fearne, Cornelia McDonald, Caroline Merrick, Constance Harrison. Their names are long since forgotten, and no one reads their diaries but scholars. These few dared, at least, to write down their treasonous views. Even if they did not condemn slavery itself, women often complained of the burdens it laid on them. They knew it was evil and un-Christian and that it deprived white women of the very ease it was supposed to provide. And though few of them have much to say about it, they also knew that white men loved black women, had children by them, and frequently treated their mulatto sons and daughters as well as their white ones. The hatred Southern women felt for slavery mingles with their hatred of slave women.

Mary Chesnut, that most extraordinary of all Southern ladies, would have found Ellen O'Hara unbelievably tiresome. During the Civil War, Mary Chesnut kept a diary (with one fifteen-month gap that she filled in later). She herself rewrote and edited her work in the 1880s, so that it is a memoir rather than a blow-by-blow account of the war years. She was as great a lady as any to be found — a citified aristocrat who could have held her own with any English duchess of the day. The old South had an urban upper crust of predictably small size, perhaps three hundred families in all. This was the world where Mary Chesnut moved. She knew everybody who mattered in New Orleans, Charleston, Savannah, and Richmond, and she understood the limitations of women within this world all too clearly. But within the limits, Mary did as she pleased.

She was as different from the white angel as anyone could have been. For one thing, she hated the country and preferred the relative discomfort of a small town-house in Charleston or Richmond to the spacious luxury of the Chesnut country home, Mulberry Plantation. Her husband, James Chesnut, was one of the Confederate elite. He had been the U.S. Senator from South Carolina before secession, and having served under General Beauregard in the attack on Fort Sumter in April, 1861, he soon became aide-de-camp to Jefferson Davis.

Whereas most women of her class were toiling many hours each day to keep their households running, Mary was truly at leisure: that was the appeal of town life. Whereas most women were bearing and rearing a dozen children each, she was childless. Whereas most women thought or said that black people were incompetent juveniles, she looked upon them as servants and was honest in her expectations that they should take care of her. Whereas most women kept their opinions, if any, to themselves, Mary had a shrewd political mind and — if only in her diary — said what she thought.

Mary was a loyal Southerner, though not a warhawk. When South Carolina seceded late in 1860, she was not sanguine. "I remember feeling a nervous dread and horror of the break with so great a power as U.S.A., but I was ready and willing. . . ." She realized that the leaders of the state were largely fools and dullards. "One of the first things that depressed me was the kind of men put in office at this crisis, invariably some sleeping deadhead long forgotten or passed over," she wrote acidly. She read everything — Shakespeare, Molière, Pascal, Sir Thomas Browne, Thackeray, George Eliot, Dickens, Mary Shelley — and thanks to her fine private library and her own efforts, she was spared the sugar-sop education provided by Southern female academies. And what she thought about slavery is anything but what a well-brought-up Southern lady ought to have thought.

Crowded as her diary is with a thousand names and happenings, Mary could not let the subject of slavery alone. She took it as a personal affront. "I wonder if it be a sin to think slavery a curse to any land," she wrote in March, 1861. "Men and women are punished when their masters and mistresses are brutes and not when they do wrong." But she was no idealist abhorring racism. She pitied black women but hated them, too. Most of all she hated white male hypocrisy and the casual bonds that white men made with black women. As she well knew, white women who took sex so lightly would have been turned out into the streets. She wrote: "We live surrounded by prostitutes. An abandoned woman is sent out of any decent house . . . God forgive us, but ours is a monstrous system, a wrong and an iniquity. . . . Like the patriarchs of old, our men live all in one house with their wives and their concubines; and the mulattoes one sees in every family exactly resemble the white children — and every lady tells you who is the father of all the mulatto children in everybody's household, but those in her own she seems to think drop from the clouds . . . my disgust sometimes is boiling over. . . . Thank God for my country women, but alas for the men! No worse than men everywhere, but the lower their mistresses, the more degraded they must be."

She spent a great deal of her time arguing, at a distance, with Harriet Beecher Stowe about *Uncle Tom's Cabin.* She knew Mrs. Stowe was talking through her hat, and she was particularly contemptuous that she missed "the sorest spot," which is the exploitation of black women by white men — at the emotional and material expense of white women: "Oh I knew half a Legree, a man said to be as cruel as Legree. But the other half of him did not correspond. He was a man of polished manners. And the best husband and father and member of the church in the world. . . . He was high and mighty. But the kindest creature to his slaves — and the unfortunate results of his bad ways were not sold, had not to jump over ice blocks. They were kept in full view, and were provided for handsomely in his will. His wife and daughters, in the might of their purity and innocence, are supposed never to dream of what is as plain before their eyes as the sunlight, and they play their parts of unsuspecting angels to the letter."

As a prison house for the women themselves, the notion of Southern ladyhood was almost as effective as slavery. No one knew this better than Mary Chesnut. "All married women, all children, and girls who live on in their father's houses are slaves," she wrote with brutal finality.

Not even the most smitten worshiper at the feet of Southern womanhood failed to state just what his expectations were. Besides beauty and grace, he expected chastity before marriage and absolute fidelity afterward, devotion to duty, and unquestioning belief in her husband's patriarchal authority. All this might also be said of the upper-class Northern woman, but the Southern woman had one more bar to her cage. Among the patriarchal institutions she was supposed to respect, slavery was foremost. "Ah, Thou true-hearted daughter of the sunny South, simple and unaffected in thy manners, pure in speech as thou art in soul and ever blessed with an inborn grace and gentleness of spirit lovely to look upon. Such a woman can well leave to the strong-minded of her sex all political twaddle and senseless dispute about the 'Rights of Women,' " was the advice of Daniel Hundley in 1860, having heard the news, apparently, that a woman suffrage movement had got started up north.

There is another persistent theme that runs through Southern history and letters, the sexual incompetence of the truly proper, upper-class white woman. In Mary Chesnut's rage is a cry of sexual as well as social desperation. How could white women compete with black ones? Slave women were readily available, obliged in the circumstances to keep silent, legally and possibly physically helpless against the white men who wanted them. And since the

Southern lady, at least according to what her menfolks said of her, matched the Virgin Mary for reticence and purity, how willing a sexual partner could she be?

It is pointless to try to generalize about the sexual behavior of a whole class of women over a whole century. Who can know such secrets? But coldness, real or alleged, in a highborn wife neatly serves the purposes of a husband with the inclination to philander. The Georgia novelist Lillian Smith, whose most famous work, *Strange Fruit*, published in 1944, is about a white man who takes a lovely black woman as his mistress, truly believed that Southern white women had been forced into frigidity and that such female sexuality and material tenderness as still survived in the South survived in the hearts and bodies of its black women. "The more trails the white man made to back yard cabins," wrote Miss Smith in *Killers of the Dream* in 1949, "the higher he raised his white wife on her pedestal when he returned to the big house. The higher the pedestal, the less he enjoyed her whom he had put there, for statues after all are only nice things to look at."

In *The Mind of the South*, Wilbur Cash stated the case somewhat differently. The black woman, he said, had been "taught an easy complaisance for commercial reasons . . . was to be had for the taking. . . . For she was natural and could give herself up to passion in a way impossible to wives inhibited by Puritanical training." Cash thought men would go out and fight wars to protect their white wives and daughters, but black women were for the bed. Even in the South today, the old lie persists that white girls are pure, and black girls dirty, and that a youth in search of sexual training will be better off in the arms of a black woman.

"I knew all about the sexual act but not until I was twelve years old did I know that it was performed with white women for pleasure; I had thought that only Negro women engaged in the act of love with white men just for fun, because they were the only ones with the animal desire to submit that way. So that Negro girls and women were a source of constant excitement and sexual feeling for me, and filled my day-dreams with delights and wonders." So wrote Willie Morris in *North Toward Home*, his deft and honest account of his boyhood in Yazoo City, Mississippi, not many years ago. Has the current generation discarded the old myths?

* * *

Feminist historians these days like to blame the patriarchy for a whole spectrum of evils from poverty to child abuse, warfare and defense spending. The logic is that men thought up these things and keep them going, and so long as men are running the world, nothing will improve much. And yet women are superb collaborators, none more so than the good old-fashioned Southern lady. She believed what she was told, or at least kept silent about her differences. She willingly took charge of civilization, religion, and decency, doling out these benefices to her menfolk in such amounts as they could swallow. If her husband got drunk, she forgave him. If he beat his slaves, she bandaged the wounds. If he made a fool of himself, she refrained from pointing it out or even denied that he had done so. She reminded him tactfully of his duty. She never overreached herself nor displayed any ambition divergent from his. If at age fifty he regarded himself as a man in his prime and her as an old woman, she accepted this. Do Southern men and women — any men and women — still behave like this?

Mary Chesnut played the game, too, mocking herself and her kind as she did so: "So we whimper and whine, do we? Always we speak in a deprecating voice, do we. . . . Does a man ever speak to his wife and children except to find fault? Does a woman ever address any remark to her husband that does not begin with an excuse? . . . Now if a man drinks too much and his wife shows that she sees it, what a storm she brings about her ears. She is disrespectful, unwifelike. Does she set up for strong-minded? So unwomanly — *so unlike his mother.* . . . And yet they say our voices are the softest, sweetest in the world."

Growing up in Arkansas, I had never heard of Mary or

her diary and believed Ellen O'Hara to be the truth. But in the end the idea of woman as collaborator was what I couldn't tolerate about the Southern mystique. One day, as an adult, I realized in horror that the little charade between the elevator man and me had been truly evil. Poor Crip had been broken for sure, and he needed to bend me to the same wheel. Uncle Tom must have his little Eva. (Mrs. Stowe was wiser than I thought.) But unlike Crip, I had the choice of saying no.

And my mother, what of her refusal to have a maid when clearly she had one? Here were two women, with much in common, innocent as lambs concerning the potent forces of history that had placed each one where she was. Neither posed any sort of threat to the other. If Mother had dressed up and gone out six days a week or had simply sat around and let Emma do the dirty work, it would hardly have been a crime. That was what my father had intended to accomplish with his hard-earned ten dollars a week. Emma needed the ten dollars. She didn't mind hard work. But Mother wouldn't do it. Some querulous old voice from her Scotch-Irish past told her that if you enslave somebody, you do it at the expense of your own identity. The mistress is the slave of the slave. So she and Emma fished the sheets out of the washer and laughed as they pinned them on the line, ironed the shirts, and stewed the parsnips. Meanwhile, behind the rose trellis I dressed paper dolls and harassed the dog or read romances. It was an edifying childhood. I hope my daughters will learn something half as useful from theirs.

Five

The Importance of Dissimulation

A Footnote on Southern Belles

Of all the skills a Southern woman is supposed to master, managing men is the most important. She can dispense with all others if necessary. The unified field theory of the science, briefly stated, is that the first step in managing men is to be a belle. Having captured and married the man of her choice, the belle then turns into a lady. The difference between a lady and a belle is that the former has a multitude of responsibilities and hence a more solid power base, while the belle thinks only of herself. Some women become ladies without ever having been belles; some remain belles all their lives, though not always successfully. A belle, unlike a lady, however, can operate part time.

The ground rules for playing the belle were invented, or at least elaborated, in the drawing rooms and on the verandas of the old plantation South, but the belle's role, like the lady's, received a particularly thick coat of lacquer in the last part of the nineteenth century. About that time reinventing the Old South took on the status of a pagan ritual, and everybody's grandmother, no matter how plain and shy she may actually have been, was declared to have been "the belle of three counties." Thomas Nelson Page, whose *Social Life in Old Virginia* set out the qualifications for Southern lady, did not forget to describe the old-time belle: "She was exquisite, fine, beautiful; a creature of peach blossom and snow; languid, delicate, saucy; now imperious, now melting, always bewitching. She was not versed in the ways of the world, but she had no need to be; she was better than that; she was well bred. She had not to learn to be a lady, because she was born one . . . She lived in an atmosphere created for her — the pure, clean, sweet atmosphere of her country home . . . Truly she was a strange being. In her muslin and lawn; with her delicious, low, slow musical speech; accustomed to be waited on at every turn, with servants to do her every bidding; unhabituated often even to putting on her dainty slippers or combing her soft hair, she possessed a reserve force which was astounding. She was accustomed to have her wishes obeyed as commands."

Venus on Olympus could hardly have outdone her, at least as Mr. Page described her. Even the daughters of the Czar or the King of France knew how to put on their own shoes. I wonder whether Thomas Nelson Page ever saw such a person or whether he was just trying to play a little joke on his gullible Yankee readers. In any case, he got some of the paraphernalia right, even if he completely missed the point. As a period creation, the belle should by all logic have died out by now: not many young women still lurk around the Corinthian columns flirting their fans and waiting for their beaus to call or lounging at their dressing tables waiting for Mammy to do up the buttons on their kidskin boots. And yet the Southern belle has survived. Not because Southern society is unchanging but because the managerial techniques devised by the belle have proved sound. One of the inexplicable peculiarities of the human species is that females usually outnumber males and must chase them down, whereas among most other animals males invariably outnumber females and must therefore exert themselves to find a mate, usually against rough and even deadly competition.

And thus even now, all over the South, belles thrive. They turn out in the hundreds to be presented at debutante balls and grand assemblies and cotillions as authorized, anointed belles. Anointed or not, they inhabit every college campus and sorority house and the corridors of every high school. They roam up and down in their pretty little dresses or maybe their neatly ironed jeans. They look shy. They pull mirrors out of their purses and pat their hair. They do whatever else they can to attract attention without seeming forward. They speak softly, do not express any but admiring opinions about any given subject, smile. Money and social position are the least of the qualifications for being a belle. It requires instead a natural theatricality, a talent for taking on a special role in a comedy of manners that will apparently run forever, no matter how transparent its characters and aims.

Belles are not hard to recognize, though it is more than the accent that gives them away. Young women from Michigan and Idaho can be just as beautiful and studiedly feminized when they want to, but they don't go about things in quite the same way as a Southerner — or if they do, that makes them Southern belles. Southern girls invariably, at an early age, catch on to the idea that being honest with men is a basic tactical error. You cannot judge a Southern belle by what you see. She is likely to be ostentatiously charming, polite, enthusiastic, sincere, and soft-headed. That's the standard model, but there are all styles: wisecracking, predatory, corruptible. It takes a keen eye to know what the performance conceals. Sometimes, of course, it is merely vapidity masking vapidity.

What the belle is after is not love but power — using the prettiest possible weapons, she is fighting a guerrilla war.

Beauty is a valuable asset in the game but not a necessity. Brains also help, although any form of intellectuality will have to be muted or even totally concealed, depending on the situation. As in any underground operation, guile is helpful, as are a cool head and a tough hide. But it is most essential that she remember she is engaged in a covert activity, and the penalty for tipping one's hand is losing the game. This is why Scarlett O'Hara, who is so often cited as the model of the Southern belle, was not a very successful practitioner of the art. Her creator never even intended her to be. From the start, Margaret Mitchell tells us that Scarlett was incapable of keeping her feelings under wraps: "But for all the modesty of her spreading skirts, the demureness of hair netted smoothly into a chignon and the quietness of small white hands, her true self was poorly concealed. The green eyes in the carefully sweet face were turbulent, willful, lusty with life, distinctly at variance with her decorous demeanor." Scarlett is too terrifying to be a belle. I have seen sixteen-year-old amateurs in east Texas in 1979 who could out-belle Scarlett.

Being a belle has its risks, the worst of which is that she may be permanently seduced by her own propaganda. She may end up believing that she really is helpless and dumb and dependent, in which case she will cease to be a belle and become a victim. The literature of the South is piled high with the battered corpses of belles, for their strategic and evasive game has tragic potential. Of all the women Tennessee Williams has created, his failed belles are the most vivid. There is Amanda, the mother of Laura and Tom in *The Glass Menagerie*. In her Chicago tenement she is pathetic and crazy and broke; her son hates her, her daughter is lame and shy. Amanda lives on her recollection of an afternoon in Blue Mountain, her probably fictitious Southern manse, when seventeen gentlemen callers arrived all at once, and there weren't enough chairs to sit them down in. She keens their wonderful Mississippi names, "Young Champ Laughlin, Hadley Stevenson who was drowned in

Moon Lake, the Cutrere brothers Wesley and Blake, that beautiful young Fitzhugh boy from Green County, that wild Wainwright boy."

Blanche du Bois from *Streetcar Named Desire* is the archetype of all failed beauties, dreaming of lost and supposedly better days, recollecting which fraternity pin it was that she wore in her senior year at the university, mourning over her lost manor house. Her delusions and evasions, like Amanda's, are too feeble to serve against the misery of her life. Like the South, she nourishes herself on false memories. But she is one of the most touching madwomen ever invented, and even as she is led offstage to the madhouse, she takes the arm of the doctor and remarks, "I have always depended upon the kindness of strangers."

Zelda Sayre Fitzgerald was another belle who ended her days in a madhouse. As F. Scott Fitzgerald's wife, she has turned up in so many memoirs of the 1920's as to have taken on the identity of a fictional heroine. In her photographs with her husband, she might have been some Jazz Age movie queen or a character out of one of his novels. But she was no work of fiction. She came from Montgomery, Alabama, an authentic belle by all accounts, in the wild and reckless mode. If there had been no such thing as a belle, she would have invented it, and she captured a talented, handsome Northerner who could be counted on to provide one thing that all belles crave — glamour.

But in Nancy Milford's splendid biography of Zelda, another woman emerges besides the Alabama flapper and the chic young wife in her fur coat, posing with her husband on some Paris sidewalk. Scott and Zelda, two perfectly matched people — as Nancy Milford observes, they even looked alike — were to unhinge one another. They got married in 1920, and in ten years Soctt had become an alcoholic, and Zelda had begun to go incurably insane. There is, of course, no simple explanation for her madness, but one thread of it was surely her Southern origins. She was playing an ancient female role perfectly, and was an even greater success in New York and Paris than she had been in Montgomery. But along the way she discovered that she had ambitions of her own. She was a writer herself, and she showed real promise as a ballet dancer. She began to realize, apparently, that she could not exist as the adjunct of even the most successful writer in America. Glamour suddenly ceased to suffice. For a Southern belle, this must have been the most self-destructive of insights. And so she lost her mind, dying at last in a fire in a mental hospital in 1948. Not a dancer, not a writer, not a wife, not a belle.

Most belles don't come to a tragic end. In an article in *Playboy* in 1972, Marshall Frady described some of his own skirmishes, as he called them, with the ladies of the magnolia, by which he clearly meant not ladies but belles. He was out to sink the notion that belles were either adorable or desirable. Having encountered a number of them, he had observed that the greater their beauty, the greater their stupidity, self-centeredness, and manipulative tendencies. Moreover, he learned that their skills were passed on like some invidious, hemophiliac gene from mother to daughter: among their other tenacious qualities, belles are intent on replicating themselves, and they usually do. What astonished Mr. Frady most was that the classic Southern belle, in all her silky allure, believes that men exist only to serve her purposes. It is hard to believe this came as news to a reporter so perceptive as he or to the editors of *Playboy*, however accustomed they may be to marketing the reverse idea.

Belles can indeed be lethal. Not only to the men they attract or to themselves but to other women. A teacher I know in an integrated Arkansas high school described the teenaged white belle as the most seriously disruptive force in a student body that had barely managed, over the past eight years, to maintain an uneasy peace. This is a newly consolidated high school of about 1,000 students, equipped with every kind of sports facility, gymnasium, and athletic coach imaginable for the boys and the expectable number of pep squads, bands, and cheerleading teams for the nonathletes, including the girls.

As often happens, the black boys were stronger, taller, more skillful than their white teammates, and soon every varsity squad and track team was filled with black players. This, according to the teacher, had worked out splendidly. The black kids had an instant path to achievement, and the white boys had been able to take the competition in a gentlemanly way. In fact, to everyone's delight, the football team began winning championships. The blacks' edge in sports also gave them a political weapon. One year the football players brought an entire season to a halt by striking for better black representation in student government. They won, too.

But, my informant continued, for girls of either race high school is the time to forget other kinds of achievements and start competing for boys. What matters is getting elected homecoming queen or being invited to parties, buying pretty clothes. Obviously, in all such endeavors, the white girls were ahead of the blacks. They were more likely to be categorized as pretty, to have money for clothes and jewelry and hairdos, to have pleasant homes and parents who could afford to give them cars, more likely to have their families behind them with the effort it takes to get elected homecoming queen or chief cheerleader and to have the money for uniforms and long dresses and out-of-town trips. Furthermore — just as their granddaddies had feared — the white girls were, in an unadmitted way, attracting the black boys. Why not? The white girls were all well-dressed and comparatively rich and smooth. There had been no interracial dating, needless to say, but the thought had crossed a few minds. The black girls, though the teacher didn't say so, were simply being outgunned in the belle department. Hence racial animosities among the girls had become an intractable problem, with both camps attacking and retaliating and even occasionally growing violent. In an incident last winter, she said, a black girl had literally jumped on a white one in the corridor and pulled out a handful of her well-coiffed blond hair. I tried to look appropriately shocked, but I understood too well how the attacker felt.

I never made any attempt at becoming a belle, having realized in early adolescence that I had almost none of the qualifications. But I grew up watching some virtuosos. In a corner of the South as remote as Arkansas, with no particular connection to any Tidewater *beau idéal*, and in a little town such as I came from, which hardly even existed before 1880, it is a miracle that anybody had ever heard of the idea anyway. There are, after all, plenty of other ways to find a man. And yet the old notions hung as heavy in the air as the fume of Blue Waltz cologne around the cosmetic counters at the Kress store. No matter how lowly your origins or plain your person, you were expected to be a belle.

There was a nucleus of girls who scarcely needed any training, among them a natural talent named Margaret Anne. She was a glorious gold-hued redhead, tending to rotundity at the bottom unless she kept to a strict diet, but brown-eyed and agreeably diminutive. Brought up in a rather splendid home (or so it seemed to her friends), an only child with indulgent and adoring parents, she had already begun to plot by the age of thirteen how to capture a husband and remove herself from this paradise. Her mother, Lula, had been married at fifteen, and Margaret Anne had come along, as they put it, before Lula's sixteenth birthday, so the two of them enjoyed their adolescence together, scheming about bridal gowns and whom to pick as bridesmaids, though the prospective bridgerooms had barely begun to shave. What Margaret Anne wanted was not so much a husband, however, or even a lot of dance dresses and corsages or a sexual partner — though she did want all those — but independence. Some control over her own affairs. Marriage may seem an odd means to that end, but not the way Margaret Anne figured it. She knew who the boss of her house was going to be and who was going to have the fun of spending the money.

As she set out, she had the first necessity of her trade well in hand — not her beauty, which was marginal, but the understanding that her first job in life was to attract boys. Second, although she was not stupid, neither was she excessively troubled by her own intelligence or cultural yearnings, which were nil, and she knew better than to display the slightest proficiency at anything. Third, she had the quality of being unattainable, of coming from that "pure, clean, sweet atmosphere" described by Mr. Page. Fourth, she had something Page completely forgot to mention: she was pious, or appeared to be. That is the herbal bouquet for the sauce and an excellent mask for all the calculated moves that a belle has to make.

Margaret Anne never missed a Sunday at the Baptist church and following her mother's advice, she sang in the choir. It was a good way to cultivate an otherworldly image as well as to display oneself and to flirt a little tiny bit with the boys in the pews. (In addition to all these benefits, Margaret Anne naturally expected a gold star to be stuck down in the Books Above.) Her silky hair looked very nice against the navy-blue choir robe with its starched white collar. During the preaching, she kept her great serious brown eyes mostly upon the swirling locks and the flapping coattails of the preacher. When the invitation came, and the piano played "Just as I Am," and the stray lambs walked up the aisle to Jesus, her face would glow like an archangel's, and tears would gleam in her eyes. It was worth sitting through church for.

On Saturdays she used to drive around town, ostensibly doing errands with her mama, but in fact making herself visible, as she did later by herself, when she had her own car. She always knew where to find the boys, recognized every one of their old Pontiacs and Fords, knew exactly who was at basketball practice or football scrimmage and when, could have told the whereabouts of any one of fifteen boys at any time you asked her, as well as the name of every girl any particular boy had dated over the past year and where they had all gone on the date. She herself was usually going steady, but now and then she broke away. She could hug and kiss and loll and fondle in the back seat of a car for hours, but she had no difficulty controlling herself, and she only fondled the steadies. Her mother had directed her to go to her marriage bed intact, and she did.

Approaching eighteen, she decided to go after the captain of the football team, a massive, handsome, slow-witted blond named Billy Ray who liked to drink beer and go out with his buddies on weekends stealing hubcaps and drag racing. Margaret Anne naturally disapproved of his mischief-making, but she didn't frown too much. His mischief was her means of controlling him. She let him know just how much beer he could drink and how much devilment he could get into without actually provoking her to return his ponderous class ring, which was adjusted to her finger by means of a pad of adhesive tape. (She did return it, two or three times, just to teach her boy a lesson.) But though Jesus had saved her soul, she intended to save her football captain's soul only so far as she chose. What she wanted for a husband was a bad little boy — not too bad, of course — but flawed enough to be unable to do without her, someone with a dependable need to be forgiven. She understood, and gently caused him to understand, just what the trade-offs were going to be.

So they were married, and Billy Ray gave up beer for bourbon before switching to vodka. He quenched his passion for cars by taking over the local Mercury dealership, and he prospered as a salesman because he gave his customers the impression of being too simple-minded to be dishonest. For the same reason, he has made some profitable deals in real estate. He somehow got in on some Title One housing money and contracted to build a series of small-scale high-rises for poor tenants, all of them black and none with any wish to live in an apartment. He now sits on the boards of two banks and is working on a deal to develop some prime lake-shore property. In every respect, he behaves as a man of his station should — he is a grateful husband, a cheerful companion to his friends, a generous if not very interested father, and a heavy drinker who never quite goes over the edge.

Margaret Anne, now quite fat but still redheaded, has remained a belle in spite of the arrival of three children. In
fact, I have seldom seen so perfect a belle as she has become in middle age. She is always "fixed up," goes twice a
week to the hairdresser, and wears plenty of nail polish.
(She has seventy-five pairs of shoes — and handbags to
match — all lined up in a special closet which she showed
me the last time I visited her. When the heels need new
tips, she gives the shoes and the matching handbag to the
maid.) Fat or not, she wears tight clothes, but her favorite
outfits are a demure suit with a frothy blouse for day and
a pastel chiffon gown for evening.

She gives elaborate, noisy parties (catered) where all the
men get drunk. She claims to be a dedicated boozer, but
she drinks very little in public or, I suspect, in private. She
moves about these massive brawls like a queen at a garden
party. I have never heard her discuss any abstract subject
with anyone, except that occasionally she will talk politics
with the men. When she does, she takes care to display ir-
rationality and passion. In his position, Billy Ray has had
to get quite close to local politics and sometimes even woo
a congressman or senator. Margaret Anne's political acu-
men consists, therefore, in admiring the men whose favor
her husband is currently courting. Her husband's friends,
including the politicians, are all as wild about her as if she
were still sixteen. Most of them have tried to "get friendly
with her," as she calls it, but she tells me that she just gives
them a little pat on the arm, tells them they are the sweetest, dearest, best of things, and then reminds them as gently
as possible that she loves Billy Ray. She is not interested
in middle-aged men, nor reckless enough to sin with her
husband's colleagues.

Her fascination, whatever it is composed of, certainly does
not consist of wit. But she is amusing — she has raised calculated silliness to the level of an art. She never misses a
chance to tell you how scatterbrained she is or that she is
taking lessons in disco dancing or that she still has all her
pink angora sweaters from high school. She dislikes cook-

ing, but when she does cook, she makes silly things: salads with canned fruit and miniature marshmallows and shredded coconut in them; things consisting of canned beans and mushroom soup mixed together and topped off with another can of French-fried onions; green and purple jello in layers; unidentifiable mixtures baked in fish-shaped molds and decorated with pimento and green olives; pies concocted from cracker crumbs and frozen lemonade mixes and aerosol whipped cream. Her basic principle is that nothing should look like what it is, and the compliment she most wants to hear is that "it looks too pretty to eat." Billy Ray used to loathe this sort of stuff but was too intimidated to say so. Now he has grown used to it, and in any case they have a cook six days out of seven.

She appears to have gotten everything she wanted out of her marriage: several furs (in a subtropical climate), white wall-to-wall carpet in every room, and a succession of casual daytime lovers not chosen from among her husband's acquaintances or his age group. One of these young men, she confided to me, was the father of her third child. She speaks of her love affairs with giggles of innocence, for she is as indestructible a virgin as she ever was, and I am sure she fantasizes that she and her "baby boys," as she calls them with a little smile and shiver, are merely hugging and kissing in the back seat. Her eldest child is a redheaded daughter who of course sings in the choir at the Baptist church and last autumn, though a mere sophomore, was chosen homecoming queen.

Six

That Old-time Religion

Anybody who grows up in the South may have to reckon, some time or another, with being born again. When I was a child, the religious fervor of my mother's family had faded to a phantom of its old self. They did not testify about the love of Jesus or shout in unknown tongues on Sunday mornings or even read the Bible at night and say grace at table. Yet they had not quite shaken off all ties with the hard-shell faith of the backwoods.

Most people I knew went to church, even if they omitted standing up and hollering. Occasionally they would go to a revival meeting and allow themselves to be shaken by it. And if you asked them, they'd tell you it was a sin to dance and smoke and drink, even though they did all these things once in a while. They still believed in heaven and hell and in the stark truths of the Bible, though they had quit reading it. Least of all had any of them questioned the foundation of all fundamentalist doctrine: that getting to heaven was a matter of one lone, orgasmic confrontation between the soul and Jesus. After that, even if the fleshly self insisted on visiting honky-tonks or breaking half the Ten

Commandments, the soul within would one day return to righteousness, for it could never be lost.

My father, transplanted Yankee that he was, held the Baptists and their ilk in contempt. With his selective affinity for Southern culture, he slung the Baptists into some nether category of ignoramuses, along with people who put cow-dung poultices on broken bones and believed in hoop snakes. His inclination, when it came to my religious training, was to school me in Methodism. He didn't mean some walleyed, floor-stomping Methodism that had moved to town from the mountains. He meant something entirely un-Southern, with no taint of emotionalism. Something urban. A church that christened babies and sprinkled the forelocks of new members and had a minister with a tangle of DD's and LL's after his name who quoted Sir Walter Scott and Wordsworth and Browning and in any case, at the end of the sermon, did not launch into an unseemly tantrum about walking on down the aisle to get saved.

But my father's desire to turn me into a respectable Christian was much too slight to energize him, let alone me. How could he expect me to take Sunday school seriously when most often on Sunday afternoons, after we had gorged ourselves on fried chicken and cream gravy, Daddy read aloud to me from Gibbon? On the Lord's day he was almost deliberate about picking passages on the early Christians and how they had made a nuisance of themselves to the Romans. Edward Gibbon perceives the saintly band as a burden borne with commendable patience by the Roman upper classes, much as in his day the upper crust had to put up with Wesleyans and Luddites. This was the one time my father chose not to take the side of the underdog. He did not construe Christians as underdogs. They were, he knew very well, constantly trying to deprive him of his livelihood. To the Hot Springs Protestant Church Council, open gambling was the the work of the anti-Christ, and they would have liked to see all bookies in jail. Daddy could deposit me all brushed and ruffled on the front steps of the First Methodist Church as many Sundays as he cared to, but I never forgot which side he was on when it came to lions versus Christians.

Still, I was too young to join him in agnosticism, and when I slipped out of the Methodist net (my absence unfeelingly ignored by them), I fell heavily into the Baptist one. This was not because my mother had pushed me toward her ancestral faith, but because the Baptists in a small Southern town make it their business to pick up stragglers. My mother, at least while I lived under her roof, never went to church regularly. Yet she had come out of the raw old tradition. I had snapshots of her on baptizing day — forty youngsters in white sheets, up to their waists in the North Fork River and scared to death, about to be dunked by a preacher who looked seven feet tall and had hands the size of shovels. When I was a child, however, something about religion embarrassed her. Most other mothers I knew went dutifully from Sunday school to prayer meeting to Circle (where they talked about foreign missions) to choir practice to Sunday vespers, and they hauled their daughters along with them. I suspect that the women went for one another's company more than Jesus' sake, but in any case, they went.

And I began to go, too, about the time I turned thirteen — the classic moment for the fundamentalist God to bring in the sheaves. Of course, my attraction to religion had something sexual in it. The preacher at the Baptist Church, ambivalently named Vergil Luther Radley, was a massive, good-looking man of about thirty-five, swarthy, brown-eyed, broad-faced, thin-mouthed, and powerfully muscled. The effect was Laurence Olivier as Othello. Brother Radley's suits were white, his Bible black. (Surely he switched to black broadcloth in the winter, but I recall only the white.) Even if he had not been young and handsome, he was a man. Not just a man, but an actor, a dancer, a performer. To young virgins such as I, he projected an almost lurid masculinity, which I loved — not knowing why or what — but knew I oughtn't to be sensing. Most Baptist ministers kept their masculinity tucked so far back that one would have sworn they were neuters. Not Brother Radley — he flaunted it, at least from the safety of the pulpit. And under his pastorate, the church flourished.

Working with the intelligence of a *premier danseur* or a quarterback running a complicated play, he could in three quarters of an hour work himself up to the classic Baptist frenzy. To the unpracticed eye, it might look uncontrolled, but one quickly learned what to expect. I relished the performance. First, with exaggerated calm, he read the Scriptures and prayed — maybe it was Saul on the road to Damascus. Before long he'd be crouching behind the lectern, the fiery black eyes staring just over the top of it as he gripped the front edge in his right hand. "Saul, Saul," he would cry out, as though the heavens had parted, "Why persecutest thou Me?" Then he'd thrust his long fingers into his breast pocket, rip out a white handkerchief, flourish it, tamp his agonized forehead with it, and wad it up, while at the end of his other arm the Bible flapped as if he meant to lob it into the top balcony. The baritone voice, rich as chocolate, sometimes bubbled with a sob. All this gesture he enhanced by darting to and fro, leaping up, slapping the Book. And as if a gale were blowing across the altar, the thick swatch of his coal-dark hair swept across his countenance and fell into his eyes.

Finally, stepping out from behind the lectern, planting his feet on the high ground and showing himself full length to the congregation, he would raise his hands skyward and cry out, "Don't remain in the darkness of sin denying Jesus. Come, come to your savior. Get up and come on down to Him and be saved." Then Brother Radley would open his arms to receive us, while the piano began to strum, and the choir murmured, "Just as I am, O Lamb of God, I come," or "There is a fountain filled with blood, drawn from Immanuel's veins." Many would be weeping aloud, and I always trembled in my pew. I had no idea what feelings — apart from the spiritual — he was playing upon in me, and neither, I believe, did he. It was all part of the preaching art, and he was good at it. I am certain that he was a rigorously faithful husband with never a roving thought.

On Sunday morning, weak-kneed and sobbing, I did go down that aisle for him. Yes, and he folded me in those white-clad arms, briefly pressed my cheek against his heaving chest, cupped my chin in his hand, and looked into my eyes. At his gentle command, I bowed my head and listened to him pray for me, thank God for me, thank Jesus that this fine young girl had come to accept Him as her Savior and Lord.

The trouble was that I was faking. Oh, I signed the card. I asked to be immersed. I sat down on the front pew and prayed with all my strength, waiting for the proper psychic jolt. Hanging on. Tensing my muscles. Even, I recall, uttering a groan or two. But it didn't happen. Apart from my now subsiding stage fright, I didn't feel any different than I had before. Soon after my baptism in the comfortably warm font, I was elected president of my Sunday school class. Lent my enthusiastic voice to the choir. Resolved to remain a nonsmoker and a pure teetotaler. Was outspoken in my disapproval of dancing — another adult skill I hadn't quite acquired. But even as I stood in the baptismal tank with a white sheet over my swimsuit, even as Brother Radley put one hand behind my shoulders, squeezed my nose shut with the other, and laid me back in the water, I knew I was a fraud.

I didn't give up hope. Maybe I could get right with God. All it took, they said, was "conviction of sin"; that is, I had to believe I deserved to go to hell, and I did believe it. And then I had to believe Jesus could save me. And I believed that, too. But for all that, it was like memorizing the rules of golf and then, out on the green, discovering that it couldn't be done.

My profoundest struggle to be born again came a couple of years later when I decided, to my father's disgust, to spend two weeks at the Baptist church camp at Siloam Springs, in the northwestern, almost primeval, corner of Arkansas. Over the two-lane roads of the day, it was at least a five-hour drive from home. Twelve or thirteen girls and three or four boys were going to church camp, the lot of us meticulously chaperoned by a pair of young marrieds who had temporarily foresworn the privileges of matrimony in order to shepherd us to Siloam. We set off from the church parking lot early one June morning in an ancient gray Sunday school bus with "Second Baptist" in big black letters on the side. The seats had no springs, and the hot wind cut scathingly through the open windows. We sang all the way — hymn books had been provided — which kept us occupied and drowned out the ominous knocks in the engine and the horrid screechings of the transmission when, on the slightest upgrade, the driver had to downshift.

Siloam, in the New Testament, is the spring outside Jerusalem where Jesus works a miracle: he sends a blind man there to wash his eyes and recover his sight. My eyes, as I approached Siloam, were blind in some sense, too. The camp site was a leafy mountain glade traversed by a brook. In the center, green and well-tended, was a kind of campus with a large tent pitched over a wooden amphitheater built on the slope of a hill. On the other side of this lawn was a white-washed dining hall. The dormitories teetered at a distance on the surrounding hills, on stilts. Boys were well separated from the girls. Instead of toilets, there were latrines, and water gushed (sometimes) from the end of a handpump. Swimming was not allowed since one needed a bathing suit to swim, and flesh was ipso facto immoral. Shorts and slacks were also forbidden, at least for the girls. Even sundresses were classed as not nice. We slept in cots in the screened-in dormitories and had no semblance of privacy — no possibility of reading or writing letters in bed. No books. No telephones. Not even some small crossroads Jerusalem to walk to and spend a quarter at the country store. Siloam was all there was.

At six we arose, dressed beside our cots, washed our faces at the pump, and heard an hour of preaching before breakfast. Afterward there were Bible classes, followed by more preaching. Lunch was at noon, and then we had a free hour before crafts classes. We made earbobs out of shells. Supper began at five. The dining room was far too small, and we languished, starving, in long lines, relieving the tedium with a lot of nervous adolescent flirting and raucous choruses of hymns. The meals consisted of canned vegetables, along with fried potatoes, hot dogs (limp), hamburgers (fried thin and crisp), huge stacks of white bread, and gluey fruit pies. Fortunately food was irrelevant to most of us.

Preaching began again just after supper and usually lasted until ten. This was the real service. At morning and noon the preachers and song leaders were most often students from some local Bible college, but at night we had the full professional complement, including what must have been the highest-stepping, loudest revival preacher in Arkansas. He frightened me. Brother Radley was always terrifying enough, with his hoarse invocations of hellfire and his implicit contempt for most human activities conducted outside sanctuary walls. But at least he was a D.D., and he had those dark eyes. This red-faced evangelist made Radley look like an Episcopalian rector. In my inmost heart, he aroused no feeling of tenderness.

He shouted, strutted, and stamped, described all the torments of hell, including pincers and demons jamming the redhot picks right into you, under your fingernails. He claimed that right here in this fine camp half the young people who thought they were saved *weren't*. If we were really saved, we'd be down here on our hands and knees at the altar, dedicating our lives to Christian service. We'd be pledging ourselves to become music directors, especially all us talented girls, or looking to marry ministers and be good helpmeets to them, or we'd be thinking about foreign missions. We'd be searching our souls for a vocation and praying to God. Instead, what were we doing? Unmindful of our immortal souls, according to him, we were strolling off into the darkness together in mixed couples, sitting down, boy next to girl, on benches at nightfall, not even bothering to come into the tent for the service. It turned his stomach to have to say it. (I had myself somewhat wistfully observed a pair of bench sitters: a crew-cut youth holding the hand of a girl whose blond perfection clearly paralyzed him. But

they said he was a future preacher, and she was his be-
trothed.) Everybody else squirmed when he said this, as
though guilty of multiple fornication. The counsellors looked
stricken. I was relieved. This was the only charge of his
that failed to nail me to the wall.

As the days went on, and the preaching got hotter, my
soul festered. I was overwhelmed by my unholy state. I
pleaded with the Lord to flood my soul with the right feelings. How could anybody want so desperately to be born
again and not be able to slip through? The preacher said
nobody had ever been turned away. But in addition to all
this angst, I loathed standing in lines for meals. I yearned
for a real bath. It stayed mercilessly hot, and it never rained.
The mosquitoes finally died of the drought. I missed my
mother, my books, my own bed. And in the middle of my
deepest prayers my eyes would fill with pictures of strolling couples, and I would yearn to be led off into the twi-
light by one of those bad, backsliding boys.

Alas, there were no brief encounters. Life in the gulag
went on — but only for its term. On the last evening, supper turned out to be ham, green beans, and potato salad —
truly a banquet after what had gone before. I ate big help-
ings of everything, in spite of a faint metallic edge in the
meat. I wondered why the milk was warm, and drank water
instead. Then I went cheerfully off to the meeting. I knew
they had cranked up for a coda, and if Jesus didn't claim
me tonight, He never would. Tonight I meant to get religion, or else I'd bow out.

We sang more hymns than usual, and the preachers, as
expected, painted hell as hotter than usual. When at last
we stood for the invitation, I discovered I was so giddy I
had to hang on to the back of the folding chair in front of
me. "Amazing grace, how sweet the sound, that saved a
wretch like me. I once was lost but now am found, was
blind but now I see." Blind but now I see. The words
scorched me, seared me, as though I had not previously
understood the English language and now miraculously did.
I felt faint, but someone caught my arm, and I didn't fall.

Instead, my transfiguration began. The tears ran, the light under the tent turned a vivid yellow, and sobbing loudly, I battled my way down the rows and joined the throng that by now was pressing toward the altar. This was it. I had done it. *We* had done it. I felt a surge of joy that could only be the certifiable, genuine thing. I quaked and sweated. When at last some toiler in the vineyards finally led me to a chair, I signed two cards, one professing my faith in the Lord and testifying to my salvation and another stating my intention to become a missionary in Africa.

That night I twitched upon my cot — one cannot thrash on a couch so hard and narrow — trying to control my sense of elated dislocation, wishing I could sleep but disturbed by technicolor dreams whenever I did drop off. At dawn I got up and read the Bible — as the preacher had admonished us newborns to do. I drank the pump water with a drunkard's thirst and settled down to Revelations. But the words uncoupled themselves from one another on the page, and I could extract no meaning from them.

Bewildered and exhausted, I dressed and packed, then went down to wait for breakfast. Today the morning service was omitted. Bus time was eight. I had to sit down on the ground while waiting in line, and then found I could not eat. Was this rebirth? I wept waiting for the gray bus to roll up. I thought about the Africans. I figured they'd be standing in a line waiting for me, and what would I tell them? I'd be real nice. I'd hold the babies and not make a fuss if the women didn't wear blouses. Everybody would love me. Where would the mission board send me? The Congo? Nigeria? I'd go wherever they said.

The bus ride down from Siloam was as jolting and hot as the trip up, but this time nobody felt like singing. I stretched out on the long padded bench in the back of the bus and slept. I woke, occasionally, and remembered what my father had told me one time about certain tropical parasites that build their homes in people's muscles, just below the skin. I thought about leeches and tsetse flies. Kraits. Bugs that burrowed into your eyeballs and made you blind. Was blind but now I see. They liked us to come back from camp rejoicing, so our counsellors woke us up in time for a weak chorus of "That Old Time Religion" as we rounded the corner and stopped in front of the church. Brother Radley, his dark face set into a smile, was waiting to receive us. I descended from the bus, shook his hand, and wobbled into the arms of my father and mother.

I had food poisoning, of course. It set in explosively just as my anxious mother led me inside the back door. The retching was over in a few hours, but the fever lasted several days. I couldn't remember ever being so sick. I slept as if drugged for forty-eight hours. When I revived and recalled that I was now among the elect, I began to read brief passages of Charles Sheldon's *In His Steps*, which somebody gave me the night of the cataclysm. The notion of the book, which I later learned is one of the all-time best-sellers, is that before doing or saying anything, one must ask oneself whether Jesus would have done or said it, and how.

Would Jesus have drunk the glass of ginger ale my mother had just given me? Was there a Baptist position on soda pop? Mother was reading aloud from the *Arkansas Gazette*. An item on an inside page reported an epidemic of food poisoning among teen-agers around the state, which had been traced to a failure of refrigeration at Siloam Springs Baptist Church Camp. Perhaps half the five hundred campers and staff had been affected, but no deaths had been reported. "So," I thought, lapsing quickly into my rationalist mode, "the buggers let the food go bad and then fed it to us anyhow." Christlike once more, I forgave them. As my strength came back, I ceased asking Jesus about every breath I took. My heart unburdened itself of unsaved souls in the Congo and Nigeria. My hard-won piety was all gone, along with the salmonella. I continued to go to church a few years more, but if I had been reborn at Siloam, it wasn't as a Baptist.

What I did not realize was that I had had a dangerous brush with history. Years later, in search of something else, I came across a report of an 1830s camp meeting. A great revival was sweeping the American frontier in those days, from Indiana to Kentucky to Tennessee. The reporter was Frances Trollope, the English traveller whose *Domestic Manners of the Americans*, published in 1832, was a fair account of what ruffians a brand new people can be. The food was better, and the preaching wilder in her day, but Mrs. Trollope could just as well have been reporting from Siloam Springs.

"It was in the course of this summer," she wrote, "that I found the opportunity I had long wished for, of attending a camp meeting . . . in a wild district on the confines of Indiana. The prospect of passing a night in the backwoods . . . was by no means agreeable, but I screwed my courage to the proper pitch."

When she reached the spot "on the verge of an unbroken forest," she found tents of various sizes pitched in a circle, including one for blacks. [Siloam was lily-white of course, but the early frontier Baptists and Methodists welcomed everybody.] From every tent came the sounds of "praying, preaching, singing and lamentation." What caught her eye at once was a handsome youth of about eighteen with his arms round a disheveled-looking girl, "her features working with the most violent agitation." A "tall, trim figure in black" was praying and preaching, and the young man and woman soon fell forward, twitching on the straw floor of the tent. In every tent was the same scene: "All were strewn with straw, and the distorted figures that we saw kneeling, sitting and lying among it, joined to the woeful and compulsive cries, gave to each the air of a cell in Bedlam."

"Above a hundred persons, nearly all females, came forward, uttering howlings and groans so terrible that I shall never cease to shudder when I recall them. They appeared to draw each other forward, and on the word being given, 'let us pray,' they all fell forward on their knees, but this posture was soon changed for others that permitted greater scope for the convulsive movements of their limbs; and they were soon all lying on the ground in an indescribable confusion of heads and legs . . . I felt sick with horror.

"Many of these wretched creatures were beautiful young females. The preachers moved among them at once exciting and soothing their agonies. I saw the insidious lips approach the cheeks of the unhappy girls; I heard the murmured confessions of the poor victims, and I watched their tormentors, breathing into their ears consolations that tinged the pale cheek with red."

The praying and shouting went on all night. One woman shouted, over and over, "I will hold fast to Jesus, I never will let him go; if they take me to hell, I will still hold him fast, fast, fast."

But then to Mrs. Trollope's admitted astonishment, after a brief rest at dawn, "I saw the whole camp as joyously and eagerly employed in preparing and devouring their most substantial breakfasts as if the night had been passed in dancing; and I marked many a fair but pale face, that I recognized as a demoniac of the night, simpering beside a swain, to whom she carefully administered hot coffee and eggs. The preaching saint and the howling sinners seemed alike to relish this mode of recruiting their strength."

Ending her account, Mrs. Trollope makes a tart remark about the large amounts of money hauled in by the preachers, to be spent, presumably, on Bibles, tracts, and, she snorts, "all other religious purposes." Her sympathy with the camp meeting mentality was slight. Yet she caught all the essentials. Not merely the hysteria of the women and the shouts of the preachers, but the sexuality of it — of which she vigorously disapproved. She dimly sensed the sociability; it gave the eighteen-year-olds a chance to do some serious courting. She seemed not to grasp that on the frontier this was the one true form of recreation available. It terrified her to see the people jump and shout, let alone roll around on the green earth. Then to her astonishment, what had appeared to be mass psychosis vanished with the rising sun. Saints and sinners had a decent breakfast, and Mrs. Trollope went elsewhere. So, no doubt, did everybody else, for they all had other business to look after. One cannot shout and tremble indefinitely — every party comes to an end. So, having completed a ritual that was to serve the purposes of country folk for at least another century — and in particular, I believe, the purposes of women — they hitched their teams to the wagons and drove home.

* * *

What part women played in forming and preserving the frontier churches of the South in the nineteenth century and what these churches meant specifically to women may not be discoverable. Women shaped the churches in the same way men did — by joining them. And certainly the Methodist and the Baptist churches gave their women a voice, if not the pulpit. And in their state of sin and unredemption, men and women approached Christ as equals. What the churches gave back to their followers was the same for men and women — the experience of salvation, which for many believers remained the emotional peak of their lives; the certitude of heaven; a law to live by in a lawless world; and — by no means least — the society and companionship of their neighbors.

It is no mystery that fundamentalism sprang up and flourished in America — though few Baptists today might like to acknowledge their radical heritage. What the Baptists were, in fact, was the first counterculture in America. No hippie in the 1960s ever aroused more wrath among the righteous — violent, overt wrath — than the Baptists did in the eighteenth century. Among all American dissenters they have the oldest pedigree and certainly one of the most honorable. The founder of the Baptist church in America was that celebrated libertarian of our schoolbooks, Roger Williams. Williams had emigrated from England to Boston in 1631 and had quickly made a public nuisance of himself by stating, among other opinions, that a civil magistrate had no right to enforce church law. In the Puritan theocracy, where church membership and citizenship were synonymous, this notion was not only heretical but treasonous. On other matters, too, he held offending views, but ultimately the most offensive of them was that the church and state ought to be separate. No one, least of all the Puritans, had yet contemplated the separation of church and state. By 1635, they had secretly arranged to transport Williams to England, where he would have stood an excellent chance of being hanged. But with the help of some Indian friends, he fled to Narragansett Bay, to found, in 1636, in his new town of Providence, the first Baptist Church in America.

In 1639, in a momentous step, Williams publicly repudiated the baptism he had received as an infant in England and had himself immersed. In so doing, Williams proclaimed that no priest or minister could confer salvation, least of all to an infant, and that the believer who had attained salvation through faith — the only way it could be attained — ought to follow Christ into the waters of the Jordan. The rejection of infant baptism and the insistence on full immersion (not as a sacrament, which is the gift of the church, but an act of will by the believer) has been one distinguishing mark of the Baptist church ever since.

Infant baptism is one of those doctrinal points that may appear fussy and trivial to an outsider or a nonbeliever but that has the power to destroy a whole institution. If, by the law of God and man, every parent must bring a newborn child to be baptized in order to save its soul, then the church bestows salvation, and the minister has a divine role. If, on the other hand, the parents conclude that infant baptism means nothing — for what can it matter to God whether the head of an uncomprehending baby is anointed? — then where is the churchly power and the dignity of the clergy? The Baptists were not the first sect to object to infant baptism, but in America they objected the loudest. No wonder, as the numbers of the Baptists began increasing, the established clergy in both North and South inveighed bitterly against them, passed laws against them, rejoiced when armed mobs marched against them and nailed the doors of their churches shut. In 1672 the assembly of Massachusetts classified the Baptists as "damnable heretics," subject to banishment. In 1661 the assembly of Virginia, with Quakers in mind, as well as Baptists, levied fines against all "schis-

matical persons" who "out of their aversion to the orthodox established religion or heretical inventions refuse to
have their children baptized. . . ." The Baptists were regarded throughout the colonies as "radicals, and anarchists, and the enemies of the moral order."

Worse than that, they were irrepressible, the more so as
the established churches fought to repress them. All the
colonies but four (Pennsylvania, Delaware, Rhode Island,
and New Jersey) had tax-supported state churches: Church
of England in the Southern colonies and in New York, Con-
gregational in New England. They hated competition.
Nevertheless, from Rhode Island and Massachusetts the
Baptists moved into Maryland and from Maryland into Virginia, the Carolinas, and Georgia. Some Baptist immigrants came from England. By the early 1770s almost every
colony had its Baptist enclaves. The Baptist church had no
central organization; it specifically shunned any such or-
thodoxy.

Not surprisingly for such free-swinging independents,
Baptists were of several stripes. In the 1730s the first of several American revival movements, the so-called "Great
Awakening," had upended the religious life of the colonies,
spawning a group of Baptists known as the "New Lights"
or the "Separates," as opposed to the Regulars. These free-
lance dissenters made emotionality the very essence of their
faith. They hollered and stamped and clapped, talked in
unknown tongues, writhed on the ground. Anybody unwilling to leap and shout for Jesus was, in their eyes, no kind
of Christian at all. At first, they did not quite discard the
old Calvinist notion that salvation was reserved only for
the elect, but it was the Separates who moved toward the
truly radical position that every man, woman, and child —
regardless of race or creed — was qualified for salvation.

For the one central, unvarying experience of this faith —
salvation — was that single confrontation of the soul with
Jesus, the same confrontation I myself would labor so hard
to achieve in another place and time. Furthermore, though
this experience most often occurred under the heavy exhor-

tations of a preacher and in the presence of witnesses, it could just as well be a solitary event in a copse or a hollow or a brush-arbor tabernacle, lacking both priest and altar. The preacher, if there was one, was nobody special: just an ordinary man who was using his "gifts." The innovation of the New Lights was to say, in fact, that any man could preach, with or without an education, but without was better. By denying the validity of infant baptism, Williams had abolished the church. Now the New Lights abolished the clergy as well.

And for the Baptists another principle had taken shape to which they still adhere — the idea of the Supreme Book, the literal, ungarnished truth of the Scriptures. No holy writ but the Bible was needed, and no philosopher from the Harvard Divinity School was required to parse it. Like the confrontation with Christ, the confrontation with the Bible became a one-to-one affair. A young woman in a sunbonnet and dirty dress who moved her lips as she read and went from one word to the next with the aid of her index finger was as well qualified to read the Book as a frock-coated scholar. Better qualified, in fact, because she was in closer touch with God. And if she couldn't comprehend all she read, the Lord would send her light.

By the eve of the American Revolution, there were many other fundamentalists at large besides the Baptists, many with similar basic beliefs. The Methodists, that other powerful church of the backwoods and frontier, had gotten their start in New York in the 1760s. The Presbyterians, too, had their ranting and shouting branches, though the church itself moved with the greatest reluctance into the backwoods. The new religions flourished especially in the South, where they had an instant appeal to the poor and the slave and to the Scotch-Irish out in the Virginia and Carolina upcountry who had abandoned the stern Presbyterianism of their forefathers and were living unchurched, uneducated, and irreligious — motivated, perhaps, by their hatred of all things English and all that the Anglican church represented.

The record of the Baptists as American revolutionaries (though I never personally have heard a minister boast about it) is one that any Baptist might take pride in. Among the Southern Baptists, in particular, there was not a single Tory. They joined the Continental Army almost en masse. In the words of Isaac Backus, a prominent Baptist preacher during Revolutionary times, they flocked to the aid of General Washington because "the worst treatment received by Baptists comes from the same principles and persons that the American War did." Though the Baptists in their early days intended to stay out of politics, there was something rebellious, indeed seditious, at the heart of their belief. Roger Williams himself had written that "an enforced uniformity of Religion . . . denies the principles of Christianity and civility." To jail a person, let alone torture or kill him for what he believed, was repugnant to the Baptists: better to limit the power of the state to commit coercion. As A. H. Newman, their most scholarly historian, wrote in 1894, "Baptists have, from the beginning . . . regarded as an enormity any attempt to force the conscience, or to constrain men by outward penalties to this or that form of religion. Persecution may make men hypocrites but true Christians never."

Right up until the start of the war, the Virginia Baptists, as well as those in North Carolina, had received little from the hands of the Anglican establishment but ridicule, abuse, and violence. Baptist preachers were repeatedly arrested and jailed. In 1768, in Spottsylvania County, Virginia, five preachers went to jail, four of them to be held for six weeks for refusing to foreswear preaching. No wonder the Southern Baptists so quickly made common cause with Thomas Jefferson and James Madison. After the war, the Baptists played a crucial role in the disestablishment of the state church. Baptist petitions to the legislature of Virginia resulted in what Thomas Jefferson was to list one day as one of his proudest achievements: the Bill for Establishing Religious Freedom in Virginia, which was passed in 1785 after a complicated and bitter fight.

This was the foundation of the First Amendment to the Constitution, which is the enduring American expression of Roger Williams's idea that church and state must not exist as one.

By the time Americans began to roll westward they had invented a faith that was ready to roll with them. From 1784 to 1812 the number of Baptist churches in Georgia, North and South Carolina, and Virginia grew from 226 to 814, and the membership, from over 20,000 to 75,000. In Kentucky and Tennessee, which in that era constituted the frontier, Baptist congregations grew from 12 in 1784 (with only about 800 members) to 441 in 1812 with 34,000 members. Not only the Baptists multiplied and brought forth fruit. The other fundamentalists flourished as well.

In every case the congregations were small, averaging only about 77 members — so that everyone must have been on a first-name basis. They all believed that Jesus was accessible to everybody, and the thought filled their hearts with joy, made them dance and cry out. In the early nineteenth century, eyewitnesses consistently came back from the backwoods describing the "multitudes, some roaring on the ground, some wringing their hands, some in ectasies, some praying, some weeping; and other so outrageous cursing and swearing that it was thought they were really possessed of the devil." At a forest camp meeting, hundreds might seek baptism; families would pile in their wagons and drive fifty or sixty miles to get to these meetings, farther if necessary. And if the orthodox and the godly back on the east coast frowned on such carryings-on, what of it?

For Kentucky and eastern Tennessee and the western Carolinas were, in those days, a light-year away from civilization. The preachers who roamed that territory functioned without architecture or vestments. They did not crave the blessings of bishops and synods back east. Every fundamentalist practice and belief tended to de-emphasize the institutional. The Methodist ministry lived for several decades on horseback and slept on cabin floors or beneath the trees. Well into this century the average rural Baptist

preacher was unlettered and unsalaried. Like his commu-
nicants he might be a farmer and herder, and he got paid,
if at all, in food or produce or the loan of extra hands at
harvest time. Ordination was not necessary. "Bro Woodride and Bro Scott is at liberty to exercise their Gift" is the
notation on the books of one primitive church in frontier
Kentucky. Thus blessed and authorized, Woodride and
Scott, whoever they were, could begin to preach — for the
gifts came from God.

Even the great camp meetings, where hundreds might
appear, took place out under the skies. A Presbyterian
preacher named James McGready, one of the founding fathers of the old-fashioned revival meeting, described one
event at a Kentucky campground in 1799. It was a Saturday, and McGready and several others (Methodists and
Baptists) had been preaching. Sinners, McGready writes,
were "lying powerless praying and crying for mercy." Suddenly — in what sticks in my mind as the quintessential
image of the frontier faith — a little girl sat up from her
mother's lap and began to shout, as McGready reports, "O
he is willing — he is come — O what a sweet Christ he is —
O what a precious Christ he is — O, what a fullness I see in
him — O what a beauty I see in him — O, why was it that
I never could believe!" Perhaps it was hysteria, but I think
it was the voice of freedom, a new cry in the world.

For like their household goods and their music and their
tin plates and spoons, their religion was not refined but
portable and practical. A mobile, democratic, adaptable instrument for a people on the move: a church for the ignorant, the illiterate, and the poor, with substantial numbers
of slaves among the membership. It was all the connection
they had with God, society, and western civilization. It was
compatible with their lust for freedom, but it acted to keep
that lust within acceptable limits.

In 1800, when two sets of Kentucky Baptists — Separates
and Regulars — decided to reconcile their differences, they
wrote down eleven bylaws, which, after the Beatitudes,
must be as brief and clear as anything in the history of

church law. Eight of these bylaws were doctrinal points: that the Bible is infallible, that God exists in Three Persons, and so on down the line. Only three of the laws prescribe behavior. Of these, two state that the churches can keep in touch with one another as they see fit, but that each one will govern itself independently, as it sees fit. And as to the duties of the members, there is but one command, which is "to be tender and affectionate to each other, and study the happiness of the children of God in general." Not precisely the sentiments one might expect in a people who toted powder horns and rifles and prided themselves on being more ferocious than bears.

This freewheeling approach to matters ecclesiastical might well have produced anarchy. Indeed, Mrs. Trollope was sure she was looking upon anarchy bare, if not something worse. Oddly enough, what it did produce was a uniform and unchangeable faith — though the shouts may have been louder or the spasms more or less violent from one place to another. The whole enterprise calmed down somewhat as it passed through the nineteenth century, but a camp meeting in Kentucky in 1830 was pretty much the same in its reincarnation in Mississippi in 1900. Once they got hold of an idea, the Baptists and Methodists hung on.

The fundamentalist faith could be — can be —harsh and unforgiving. And yet the admonition to be tender was in it, too. As much as anything Americans have ever devised, it had the element of democracy in it. Whether or not women actually created this wondrous thing, it was destined to work in their behalf, to function, in fact, as the most useful implement they took west with them.

Quick to arrive on the fresh-turned edge of the frontier, the fundamentalists set up as primitive family courts. After preaching and praying, "discipline" was the chief business of the frontier Baptist church, and in the Southern backwoods, the tradition survives even unto this day. Discipline in the hands of churchmen can be a formidable political tool, involving dungeons and racks and redhot instruments. The rulers of Salem and the Bay Colony, for example, could put you in the stocks or stitch an A on the bosom of your dress or throw you in the town pond and see if you floated upward. The frontier Baptists coveted no such power and were in any case boisterously unsystematic. The line they drew between democracy and anarchy was fine indeed.

One of the earliest Baptist churches in Kentucky was the Forks of Elkhorn Church, on the Elkhorn river in eastern- most Kentucky. It was founded in 1788 by a pioneer named William Hickman, a famous old frontier preacher who stayed with that same church for some thirty years. Hick- man's preaching style, according to one witness, was "plain and solemn," the sound of his voice like distant thunder. "But when he became animated," the account goes on, "it was like thunder at home, and operated with prodigious force on the consciousness of his hearers." Unlike most of his ilk, Hickman was literate, if not learned. The white males in most Baptist churches met one Saturday a month to look after matters temporal, and the meticulous records that Hickman kept — from 1800 to 1820 — of these sessions at his church have survived.

White women and men, slaves, and a few free blacks are vividly in evidence in Hickman's chronicle. Among his as- sociates — he called them "helps" — Hickman had no par- ticular authority. His only honorific was "Brother," just as the other men were "Brother" and the women "Sister," though everybody, of whichever sex or color, often did without honorifics. During Hickman's pastorate, church membership rose from 60-odd to about 300. It was a mo- bile, restless population, vocal and quarrelsome, with — by my count — about as many black members as white. Every Saturday, Brother Hickman recorded the names of new members:

recd by letter Bro Thos Woldridge & wife

Recd by Experience Condorces Belonging to
Jas Saunders

Recd by recommendation Sister Frances
Mastin also by Experience Betsy Majors

Newcomers came either professing "experience," i.e., their personal experience of salvation, or with a voucher letter from a previous church or on the testimony of a current member. Nearly every Saturday a batch of members departed, bearing their own letters of "dismission" to carry to the next church. Members occasionally just quit. In a letter dated March 29, 1807, one George Brown, Jr., who lived sixty miles away, respectfully asked the church to "cratch my name out . . . for my conduct is not becoming of a professor of religion." Charity, a slave, sent word that she was living in adultery and wished to be omitted from the lists of the righteous.

Nearly every Saturday, too, some "query" came before the house: "Is it right to extend the handshake of fellowship to a new convert who has not yet been baptized?" (Answer: yes.) "Is our present mode of receiving Members right or agreeable to the principle of the Gospel?" (Shelved.) "Is the Son of God equal and Eternal with the Father?" (Majority votes yes, but — magnanimously — "Minority was call'd upon to give their reason.") "Should funds be raised for the support of Brother Hickman?" (The vote was yes, but many years passed before the committee raised the cash and set his salary at sixty dollars per annum. Queries never came up for a vote until a month or more after they were raised, lest anybody get hotheaded. Sometimes the questions piled up, and Hickman occasionally made the sage parliamentary notation, "The Query referred to this meeting from our last, throw'd out."

But the real business of every session was not membership or doctrine but discovering and admonishing the backslidden. The ultimate weapon against bad conduct of any sort was exclusion from the church. This may sound sour and harsh, yet exclusion did not imply damnation (that being God's prerogative) nor loss of citizenship (which was guaranteed to white males by the Constitution). Members called to account could speak their minds, and excluded members who repented could be quickly readmitted. Exclusion required a two-thirds vote, and anybody who felt ill-used was at liberty to lodge a complaint against the entire church body. Nearly everybody, including the preacher, got in trouble at one time or another. The two-way traffic on and off the church rolls must have been heavier than on the Cumberland Road, and the defiant goats probably outnumbered the lambs in the fold. Somehow, nevertheless, the system worked.

To one who has sat, as I have, in the laced-tight atmosphere of an urban Baptist church, where holiness is as thick as fog and human sinfulness can be mentioned only by careful indirection, the openness of the discourse in backwoods Kentucky is amazing. People out there were dedicated hell-raisers, and they didn't mind saying so. By far the greatest number of citations were against white men. Their besetting sin was the bottle. In frontier Kentucky men, women, and children drank whiskey at one time or another. The Baptists were not teetotalers in those days. But at some point the brothers and the sisters had to draw the line. The first misdemeanor Brother Hickman recorded, in April, 1800, was "The Charge against Bro Wm Ballard Brot by Bro Cash for Drinking to an excess." The matter was held over until the next meeting, which took place in July, at which time "Bro Ballard appeared before the Church made acknowledgements of his fauts and the Church acquitted him." Again and again, monotonously, the poor drunkards were hauled into committee session. "Fighting" was often added to the charge of excessive drinking. Swearing and cursing, along with drinking and fighting, were also grounds for exclusion.

At one time or another every vice of the frontier — or almost — came parading into the little churchhouse: "Drinking too free and fiteing," "Immoral Conduct," which undoubtedly meant some sexual transgression. In addition to being drunk and disorderly, Brother Baker Ewing had been "misusing his wife": beating her, no doubt. He was tossed out (whereupon he may have beaten her even harder, but at least his conduct fell into the criminal category). Men were called up for horse racing and gambling, shooting for liquor, frolicking and dancing, stealing and lying, sharp practices in horse "swaping." In some cases the church mercifully agreed to "bear with" the miscreant. But sometimes it booted him unceremoniously out. Sometimes it dispatched a committee of sisters and brethren to reason with the sinner, especially in the case of drunkenness. One sufferer, Brother Ross, came up several times on the sousing charge. On one occasion, he repudiated ("repubated") his own "miss Conduct" and was forgiven. Another time, failing to show up in a repentant frame of mind, he was excommunicated.

The black membership, both slave and free, came in for its share of chastisement, though not so often as the free white males. There is no way of knowing what other kinds of punishment the slaves may have gotten besides exclusion from church, but Hickman and his helps dealt with them as evenhandedly as they did the whites. Like white males, slave men and (less frequently) women were cited for heavy drinking, lying, stealing, and immoral conduct. Adultery was sometimes hung around the necks of black men; the committee had some troubled conversation about whether a slave, forcibly sold away from his wife, could marry another. The answer was no. The black women bore a disproportionate share of "morals" charges. One slave, Hannah, was expelled for "whoredom," and Clary, "for being too intimate and sleeping with Joe." One "Vina," whose race was not specified, was thrown out for adultery. Sarah, a free black, was called up for thieving and lying; she was convicted. A while later, justice was invoked against her husband Robert as an accessory to the crime.

In one case that proves, astonishingly, that slaves could and did speak their minds, Sister Esther Winney, a slave woman, was ejected from the congregation on account of her mouth. She had announced to the world at large that she no longer felt it her duty, since her conversion to Christianity, to serve her master and mistress: if they had been Christians themselves, they would not have kept Negroes, and furthermore, in her opinion, "there was thousands of white people wallowing in Hell for their treatment to Negroes — and she did not care if there was as many more." Hickman calmly referred the matter to the next meeting and then excluded Sister Esther. Nothing is in the record to show that this rebel endured any further punishment. Slaves did, once in a while, come in and complain of mistreatment. A Brother Palmer took to task a man named Stephens and his wife for putting their slave Nancy in irons and then lying to the church about her. One slave woman accused her owner of threatening her with a whipping. She in her turn was accused of lying, and the charge was made to stick. Maybe she got the whipping later, but the fact that she came at all must mean that in this church, at least, brutality toward black members was not taken lightly.

The Forks of Elkhorn Church, and indeed all frontier Baptist churches, were ill at ease over the question of slavery. One of the early abolitionist groups in America was the Friends of Humanity, created in 1807 by dissenting Kentucky Baptists. They thought slavery was contrary to Christian principles and "the existing laws of this commonwealth." They refused to admit slaveholders to Christian fellowship — with a few exceptions: if the slaves in question were too young or too old or too ill to be emancipated and if the owner treated them humanely and legally recorded his intention to emancipate them if circumstances ever permitted. The abolitionist wives of slaveholders were also welcome, whatever the opinions of the husbands.

Brother William Hickman was not a member of the Friends of Humanity, but he hated slavery, and on the second Saturday of September, 1807, raised a major ruckus in the Forks of Elkhorn Church by abruptly informing the membership that "he was distressed on account of the practice of Slavery as being tolerated by the members of the Baptist Society and therefore declared himself no more in Union with us." Of course they excommunicated him. He had had a close brush with exclusion the year before. Preacher Carter Tarrant, one of the founders of the Friends to Humanity, had been expunged from the rolls of *his* church for his abolitionist activities, and Brother Hickman had invited Brother Tarrant home with him. At this, Hickman's helps called him to the bar of justice on charges of entertaining an excommunicated preacher. They acquitted Hickman by a vote of eight to five, but the slavery question rankled. Eventually, in 1845, the Southern Baptists took a proslavery position and split off from the Northern branch — a division that endures to this day. Brother Hickman, whatever his private feelings, did not choose to remain a schismatic forever. In 1809 he returned to preach at Forks of Elkhorn Church once more.

What did the work of the church mean to the women, specifically? No woman (white or black) ever served on the business committee, but they were conspicuous as church members. Both black and white women often entered and left the church rolls. The slaves and free blacks were invariably so identified, but by no means all the white women came under the category "& Wife." Their names were everywhere. To take four random examples: who were Nancy Berryman, Ruhana Thompson, Agnes Smith, and Lucy Ramsey? Widows, spinsters, independent wives? They arrived and departed alone. One thing is sure: though they were not blameless, the white women appeared far less often than anybody else in the ranks of the chastised.

There were, certainly, a couple of citations for drunk and disorderly. Sister Peake or Peek was a heavy imbiber, but after a visitation committee went out to reason with her, her name remained on the lists. Betsy Hicklin had her membership revoked for leaving the church "in a disorderly way." Sister Polly Edrington was hauled up for "frequently giving her Mother the lie and calling her a fool and for Indeavouring by Tattleing to set several Neighbors at Strife with each other." She was excluded. Sister Hicklin got back in the ecclesiastical good graces after patching things up with Sister Stephens, who had apparently provoked the "disorderly" leave-taking in the first place. Only black women were summoned on morals charges (though never for any interracial relationship). Whatever the reasons, in this society where women must surely have had many chances to stray, not one white woman was ever summoned to account for adultery or fornication. Were their menfolks reluctant to accuse them publicly? Did they invariably manage to remain virtuous? Did no white women ever "get too intimate" and take to sleeping with Joe? From what I know of Baptist farm women, they may have been a fairly straight-laced group, even on the Kentucky frontier. But perhaps the Baptist church, even while the men meted out discipline and decided what was what, was working for the white women, not against them. When one group takes all the punishment while another escapes, the reason may be that the scot-free group is somehow in control of the situation.

These pioneer women were certainly not weak or timid, though in Kentucky in 1800, as in Arkansas in 1900, women had no more legal rights than slaves. In this wild, dark place with no visible sign of social amenities except for a primitive church, even the strongest women must have been grateful for some help in the discipline department. A woman with several small children, living in a log cabin ten miles from the nearest neighbor, what was she to do if her husband took to drink? Where would she turn if he beat her up and thrashed the children? If these scores of penitent and impenitent brawlers excluded from the Forks of Elkhorn Baptist Church were noisy enough to attract the notice of their neighbors, they must have been murder on their families. With no civil authority to protect her, a woman could at least swear out a kind of warrant in church. For their part, perhaps the sinful males, struggling with wild animals and Indian attacks and rocky homesteads and trying not to consume the entire produce of their stills under the circumstances, did not mind having a place to go for confession and a little help from their friends in controlling self-destructive impulses. The slaves surely did not object to having a forum for their woes and transgressions, alleged or otherwise. Could Sister Esther Winney have shouted defiance in the streets of Savannah?

By the early years of this century when my grandma Lavisa Eugenia was rising on Sunday mornings and packing
her family off to the Baptist church in Buckville, Arkansas,
religion had become slightly less quarrelsome. Another
change was that the congregations were segregated. Yet I
believe the church she belonged to was essentially the same
as the one at the Forks of the Elkhorn River in Kentucky,
and that the purposes it served for rural women were similar all over the South.

On a Sunday morning, say, in March, 1914, Lavisa would
have been forty and the wife of Andy Loyd for some eight
years. That day she had eleven children in her household:
her two from the sod house in Oklahoma, her husband's
motherless five, and four born since, including seven-month-
old twin babies, one of them Velma, who became my
mother. The babies slept in a trundle bed beside their parents in the back bedroom, and Lavisa would have been up
at dawn to nurse and dress them — after she made a trip
to the outhouse, drew a bucket of water from the well, and
washed. In the big front bedroom, with its scrubbed pine
floors and muslin-curtained windows, nine children would
be sleeping, their bodies strewn on the four double beds
that stood in each corner. Sleeping in the middle was the
worst.

Mr. Loyd got up when Lavisa did, dressed, and vanished
out to the barn. All the children except the babies were old
enough to work, and soon they would be up and out, dressed
in jackets against the spring chill, hurrying across the
breezeway to the kitchen, drawing water for breakfast,
starting the blaze in the stove, carrying kindling and
dumping it into the kitchen hopper, fetching milk and butter from the springhouse, shaking the feather tickings and
remaking the beds. Though the sweet gum trees and the
oaks outside would be in full green by this time, the fire
would feel good. Next month everybody could start going
barefoot, and the jackets would go into the cedar chest. But
now everybody tried to find jobs to do in the warm kitchen,
and there were plenty: the babies to mind, sausage and ba-

con to fry, gravy to make in the pan afterward with plenty of flour and sweet milk, three or four dozen biscuits to shape and set in the oven, eggs and potatoes to fry, coffee to set boiling, molasses to dip up into a pitcher. And then, of course, came the cleanup: leftovers dished up and covered with a cloth at the center of the table, every plate and cup and fork and pan washed and dried and set back on the shelf, and the floor swept and washed so that half an hour after the family had breakfasted, the kitchen looked exactly as it had before everyone had arisen.

Next it was time to dress. Mr. Loyd had put on his clean shirt and overalls when he arose and had been careful not to dirty them as he went about his chores in the barn. For the twins, Mrs. Loyd had white dresses and sweaters and booties and caps. She no longer remembered which babies had worn them first. Each daughter had a good cotton dress and woolen jacket, each son his fresh-ironed shirt. All thirteen in the household had bathed the night before, in water heated on the wood-stove and poured into a galvanized tub. But this morning, Lavisa might insist that every neck, ear, face, and pair of hands must be rewashed and line the little ones up and apply a rough washrag and homemade soap. By nine o'clock when Mr. Loyd drove the wagon and team of mules to the side of the house, and Mrs. Loyd tied her bonnet and picked up her babies and her Bible, nothing had been left undone. All nine children had their shoes tied and looked decently clean, the twins had been fed again and were content and sweet-smelling, not so much as a nightcap or bit of dust was on the floors, and the quilts were neatly folded at the foot of each bed. If anybody's toes were pinched in hand-me-down shoes, or if any of the girls envied a sister's dress, or anybody's shirt collar was starched too stiff, or anybody's back ached from overwork, nobody made any noise about it. And now, instead of heading out to some harsh, hot task in the kitchen or the fields or walking the long road to school, everybody set off to see friends and shout and praise the Lord. Not a bad trade-off.

The service was always the same: singing, preaching, testifying. If the preacher were sick, or if there were no preacher temporarily, singing and testifying would be all of it. Sometimes the whole lot of them would go down to the black church in the next village, or, similarly, be joined by the black congregation if that church were preacherless. In 1914, the Buckville church would not yet have had its piano, that tuneless upright they still use once a year on Decoration Day. In Lavisa's time, they sang unaccompanied or with whatever rude instrument was at hand: Lavisa played the accordion sometimes. Sometimes a gospel quartet performed. The testifying was unrehearsed, and however incoherent it may have been, focused on the central experience — the soul in touch with Jesus. According to the people who can still recollect these days, the women got especially loud and tearful at testifying time and even talked in strange tongues. Lavisa, they say, sat straight on her bench, never lost control and shouted. She had too much dignity to carry on like a Holy Roller.

The preachers certainly preached hellfire, and when the church committee met, it tossed the backslidden into outer darkness and refused to take them back until they repented. After a revival, the local Justice of the Peace would be busy for days, recording the oaths of newly reclaimed Baptists who swore never again to drink or smoke or dance. And yet when the survivors meet to talk of these faraway times, what they recollect are the festivals: the thousand or so colored eggs hidden on Easter Sundays, the all-day singings, the sumptuous picnics on the grounds, the pleasures of the big baptizings that lasted all day, the Christmas Eve parties, children's Sunday every spring. "Be tender and affectionate to each other, and study the happiness of the children of God," was how the old commandment had originally read in those first frontier churches. And thus here, in a clearing in the Arkansas forests, the Baptist church functioned not merely to chastise the downfallen and terrify the unredeemed. It functioned as an instrument of love. Ultimately, however, its earthly gifts — as differentiated from its spiritual ones, which I am not qualified to measure —went beyond mere sociability or even orderliness.

Something in the fundamentalist experience worked to redefine what a man had the right to do. Worked, in fact, to redefine masculinity. The process began with the very experience of personal salvation. Christ was divine but a man as well: bleeding and chaste but still a man. The metaphor of salvation — giving in to Christ, submitting to his will, accepting Him as Master — came naturally to women. Salvation was and is a poetic transformation of a relationship that women learn from early childhood. They trust and obey their fathers, look to their brothers for protection, and then become wives. Becoming the bride of Christ is not part of a man's training. Washed in that fount of blood, he will never be purely masculine afterward. Out in the wilderness in the nineteenth century, women surely realized that to get a man to kneel down before Christ was the first step in domesticating him and taming him.

American frontiersmen, north or south, were about as barbaric and wild as human beings ever become. And the Southern white man (close, even in his civilized state, to rural ways) has traditionally been wild and cussed, even in his most admirable conformations. In almost every account of him, he emerges as a rough customer. He fights, duels, gambles, drinks hard, understands horseflesh better than human flesh. *Gone with the Wind,* that index to Southern female types, contains some archetypical Southern males as well — none of whom, incidentally, are in any way religious. Early in the book, Margaret Mitchell neatly defines the masculine mystique: ". . . here in north Georgia, a lack of the niceties of classical education carried no shame, provided a man was smart in the things that mattered. And raising good cotton, riding well, shooting straight, dancing lightly, squiring the ladies with elegance and carrying one's liquor like a gentleman were the things that mattered."

She is speaking of Brent and Stuart Tarleton, the red-haired twins who sit at Scarlett's feet in Scene One and later ride off to die at Gettysburg. They are the embodiment of one kind of Southern masculine mystique. Ashley

Wilkes, of course, cares little for the things that matter. He exemplifies some of the classic traits, in fact, of the well-bred Northern lady. He is dreamy, passive, and avid for book-learning and music. Rhett Butler, the great romantic hero of the book, can certainly do all the things that matter when he wants to, and he does do some of them. But somewhere, somehow, he has managed to become an adult and consequently is even more male than the Tarleton twins or Ashley. Among other things, he ruins the reputations of silly girls, befriends a whore, makes mad dashes through the Yankee blockade. He even gets drunk and rapes his wife. (She loves it, as the heroines of all such novels must.) Margaret Mitchell, for all her skill at creating strong female characters, did not think too well of the domesticated male.

Five years after *Gone With the Wind* had appeared, Wilbur Cash, in *The Mind of the South*, wrote his famous description of the Southern man — the "man at the center," who was as devoid of piety as Ashley or Rhett. Cash's man was a mindless, bourbon-soaked specimen, not too different from his primitive Scotch-Irish ancestors, a creature who ran "unpremeditated foot races, wrestled, drank gargantuan quantities of raw whiskey, let off wild yells and hunted the possum; because the thing was already in his mores when he emerged from the backwoods, because on the frontier it was the obvious thing to do, because he was a hot stout fellow, full of blood and reared to outdoor activity, because of a primitive and naive zest for the pursuit in hand." He was violent. He went in for knife fighting and eye gouging — not in self-defense but because he liked such things. He was, Cash said (apparently forgetting which side won), the best fighting man in the world: ". . . the thing that sent him swinging up the slope at Gettysburg on that celebrated, gallant afternoon was before all nothing more or less than his conviction . . . that nothing living could cross him and get away with it." A generation and a half later, in *Southern Ladies and Gentlemen*, Florence King detected almost the same traits in the typical Southern male of our day but added one thing that Margaret Mitchell and

Wilbur Cash merely hint at — that he is perpetually horny.

All this, I believe, veers somewhere in the vicinity of truth. In any case, it is virtuoso mythologizing. Yet that male wasn't the archetype looked to by Eliza McElroy or Lavisa Loyd or a million other Southern farm women who had better things to do than to watch a wild man cut capers or to pull the boots off him when he got drunk. And in their quest for a good man, the Baptist church was an ally, for the fundamentalist religions, Baptist or Methodist, required of the man that he come to the front of the church and speak out about his faith. They insisted that he alone was responsible for his actions. They scrutinized the backslider in a painfully specific way and did all they could to civilize him. If a man went out boozing and whoring on Saturday, sooner or later some Sunday he would be thrown out of church. The system was not ironclad. Many men did exactly as they pleased and lived with the consequences, but in a community where there was no such thing as a stranger, the church served its purpose well.

And so when Andy Loyd hitched up the team and rode off to church beside his wife, anybody in the county could look at him and know that he was *good*. Andy wouldn't have cut much of a figure in the plantation South, or in Virginia. He didn't fight or drink (except some ferociously potent eggnog at Christmas). He never gouged any eyes or let out wild yells. He was a fair hand at growing cotton, and he shot straight enough to have been of some use at Gettysburg. Had he been required to serve there, he would have gone but would not have felt gallant for doing it. If he hunted possum, it was for the cookpot. He worked hard, took his eldest boy and girl to town every fall and bought them shoes, and saw that every Christmas stocking had an orange in it. If he swore, it was behind the barn. Whether he chased women or not, I don't know, but I doubt it. When some Southern women I know speak of a good man, they mean Rhett Butler or even that good ol' eye-gouger that Wilbur Cash loved. But when women in the rural South used the term, they had someone like Andy in mind.

Seven

Generations

The legacy passed from mother to daughter is everywhere
ambivalent and complex, full of unconfessed wishes and
unadmitted bequests, woven with demands and admoni-
tions, some of which contradict the rest. In the South, with
its lady myths combined queasily with the half-forgotten
attitudes of the frontier, the contradictions draw the reins
taut. The advice that most mothers pass on, though usually
not in direct discourse, is that men are the enemy: a pack
of Yankees. Treat 'em sweet, and talk real nice to 'em, but
don't ever forget what they are. If that sounds like some
mutant form of radical feminism, it isn't. If the women's
movement of the 1970s has passed right over their heads,
however, it is not because Southern women are dimwitted
or born reactionaries with the code for Total Womanhood
strung along every chromosome (as outside observers
sometimes like to claim) but because this complicated legacy passed from mother to daughter sternly forbids open
confrontations. I have had a while to think about my own
mother's legacy — she died twelve years ago, at the age of
fifty-four, and although I am not sure I understand, or ac-

cept, what she passed on to me, I can't lay it aside, either. It has begun to acquire its own patina.

Like many women these days, at least in New York where I now live, I have spent many a noon and midnight talking about my mother. (Women talk about their mothers in the South, as well, but are less systematic about it. This is because of the Southern scarcity of psychoanalysts, whose services down there are generally reserved for the certifiably insane.) The perennially agonizing subject of Mom has turned into a kind of media fad in the Northeast, second only to jogging and lodged in the same self-improving category. Mothers don't get much credit from their daughters anymore. Many women regard their mothers' ideas as trite and irritating; their notions of morality, obtuse. The sore point is almost invariably sex. In the aftermath of the sexual revolution, Mother, poor girl, turns out not to have been revolutionary at all — a loyalist, rather, to the *ancien régime*.

Nancy Friday's best-seller *My Mother, Myself* is one recent expression of this view. Writing in the first person plural, a syntactical device intended to be as all-enveloping as mother love, Ms. Friday speaks not of her mother but "our mother," or even plain "mother," as if we all had had the same one. Mother is a fairly chic and even sexy lady; she may even be totally frank, the sort who would ask us out to lunch to discuss her private life and then go shopping with us at Bergdorf's. But watch out. For all her apparent camaraderie, Mother sees us as a sexual rival. We'll grow up and take her man away, or maybe take him even before that. Out of spite, envy, or good intentions (the ugliest of motives), Mother deliberately teaches us to undervalue sex. She may herself be emotionally underdeveloped, may not know or care about multiple orgasms or therapeutic masturbation. And if she does know, we daughters will be the last she'll tell. However, with the aid of our psychoanalysts and lovers, according to Nancy Friday, we can nevertheless break out of Mother's constricting mold.

On the surface, at least, my mother was totally unlike the

one described by Nancy Friday. Indeed, she was such a throwback to another time as to have taken on a quality of uniqueness by now. She was unlike any of my friends' mothers, too, the friends I have made in the North as an adult. Sweet-natured, generous, and ingenuous as she was, she came out of a tradition, pathological if you will, that could ask a woman to bear a dozen children before the age of thirty-five and watch over the matings and birthings of livestock and yet expect her never to have one word to say about any of it. My mother managed to get off the farm and to sidestep the quota of children, but she never abandoned the code of reticence.

This code was so stern that mothers routinely failed to pass on the simplest kinds of information to their daughters. Nobody would say a thing. My mother's oldest sister, Vera, did not learn what menstruation was until her elderly great-uncle explained it. He had found her one afternoon weeping behind a tree, bleeding and almost suicidal. (She told me the story years later in the tones of one who had been rescued at the last minute from drowning.) According to the tribal wisdom, women were supposed to learn from experience, not words. If they went into marriage and childbirth with any but the haziest notions of how their bodies worked, it was no fault of their mothers.

This lunatic stoicism did not arise from any genteel Victorian sources or any borrowed notions of upper-class ladylike prudishness — though the results were sometimes the same. It was fostered, if not invented, in the harsh sermons of Methodist and Baptist preachers who always labored to iron any pleasurable wrinkles out of life, not too hard a job in the Southern backwoods. But its real source was partly that these farm women were unwilling to think of their femininity as any kind of special condition in need of discussion. Sex was like the seasons of the year. What was there to discuss? In any case, monthly backaches or pregnancy hardly disqualified you from milking the cows or doing the wash, so why think about it? The one piece of information that was invariably spelled out, usually by means of some parable about a local sinner, was that sex before marriage was unthinkable. After marriage, it was a regular and possibly comic nuisance, tolerable enough except that it kept you pregnant. If you could think of a way to confine it to alternate Tuesdays, you did.

This was roughly my mother's attitude, at any rate, and her mother's, which she somehow transmitted to me without saying much about it. One way that Mother and I communicated was by going to the movies. We went often. This was the late 1940s and early 1950s, the golden age of cinema so far as Mother was concerned. In the land of Bing Crosby or Betty Grable, romance was romance and had nothing to do with bed. Like executions in the classic French theater, sex took place offstage. If at all. What appealed to Mother about these movies was the fluff — no dirty dishes, no bills, no babies. Once, in an Olivia de Haviland-John Lund film we saw together, called (I think) *To Each His Own*, the romance somehow produced an illegitimate baby, and my mother emerged into the late afternoon sunlight shaken and appalled. She could hardly look me in the eye; I felt I ought to pat her hand and soothingly explain the facts of life to her. Nevertheless, I got the drift of her thinking on unwed mothers. Perhaps her puritanism harmed my personality; I don't know. At the age of ten or eleven I came across my father's rare edition of Casanova's *Memoirs*, a most instructive work with excellent line drawings. Like any halfway intelligent child, I figured things out on my own. Not to minimize, of course, the information my older cousin also supplied.

My mother's peculiarly hard-shelled innocence makes her an extreme case. Southern women certainly are not too prudish, as a class; nor was she a prude. But she had her rule of silence, and she observed it. Nevertheless, she taught me amply. Children learn what they learn about grown-up life not from preachments but from inference, as if they were studying the habits of birds. In every house are secret places — bureau drawers, for example, apparently filled with shirts and socks but that prove, as a child's hand probes them, to shelter old letters at the bottom; a hinged-top box that holds a few odd pieces of department store jewelry but also a collection of five silver dollars, laid away against some eventuality ("Can I have them, Mama?" "No, and stop prowling around my dresser drawers!"); a box of old rent receipts and in among them a photograph of a woman; and those crannies — up high or locked away — where one's parents keep the paraphernalia of their private lives. In the bottom of the little table beside my parents' bed was a drawer, once lockable, but the lock had broken. On afternoons when Mother was safely outdoors hanging up the wash, I used to bring my cousin to look into it. Inside the drawer, under an old silk scarf, were a tube of jelly and an applicator; even at age eight I instantly understood their category if not their precise use.

The drawer, of course, was forbidden territory. My mother knew that I looked into it now and then, but she could never admit that I did. Nor could she admit that I knew about the bottle of whiskey in the top of the pantry, from which, after I had been tucked away in bed, my father sometimes poured an ounce for each of them, on nights when the tube and applicator were also to be required. It was the only occasion that called for a drink. Both the bottle and the tube were apparently inexhaustible. I don't recall my father smuggling packages into the house. Cleaning out that pantry after Mother's death, I found a fifth of bourbon one quarter full — it looked like the same old bottle — and I drank it.

As I grew to adolescence, I imagined, from closely observing the boredom and vexations of matrimony, that the act my parents committed and the one I so longed to commit must be two different things. What young lovers did had to be transcendent. I was too ignorant to construct detailed fantasies — nothing mechanical, no expert foreplay, no manipulation, no insertion. I envisioned a diffuse, ecstatic act, divinely lighted from above. Jupiter and Danae. The rape of Leda. Whatever Scarlett and Rhett had done at the top of the stairs. Coupling, I figured, must be the central fact of life. Beside it all ambition paled. What could a college degree mean by comparison with such an act? How could anybody hold down a job? Make a home? Go to the polls and vote?

I yearned to be perpetually in someone's arms, discovering those mysteries that I assumed were endless. Yet here was my mother, unable even to speak of such a thing except to warn me, in the discreetest terms, of its life-destroying consequences. In her atlas the road from sexual congress to the Home for Unwed Mothers was swift and straight. One day when I was about sixteen, I came into her bedroom and found her cleaning out the drawers. "Stay awhile," she said, so I sat down and watched as she arranged, folded, inspected, discarded.

Then quickly, as in a sudden acknowledgment of my years, she pulled open the night-table drawer and emptied it on the bed. Quite deliberately she took the tube and applicator and threw them into the brown bag with the rubbish. "Well," she said, — and I knew she was referring to sex, not to the apparatus — "I'm thankful not to have to put up with *that* any more." Put up with it? This blissful dream that woke me from my sleep on summer nights in time to watch the moon go down? What to me was ineffable, to her was a mere nuisance, something one should hope eventually to be rid of. If there is one thing that seems characteristically Southern about the attitudes she wished to pass along to me, it is that sexual passion is not something holy and transcendent but something commonplace, at best; not ecstasy unalloyed but, in the long run, something dangerous and certainly not a reliable foundation for one's feminine self-esteem. The day she threw the jelly in the trash she could not have been more than thirty-seven. It is enough to bring tears to the eyes of Masters and Johnson, and it would give Nancy Friday's psychiatrist the creeps.

In other ways besides her reticence, my mother was in step with an older ethic. She was born in 1913 and was closer to the nineteenth century in most ways than to the twentieth. My daughters will not be quite thirty when the twenty-first century begins, but my mother's soul was formed in that other era. She and her twin brother Delmar were next-to-the-last of five children in a houseful of older half-siblings. As twins, Velma and Delmar got more petting than one baby would have, but the attention had to be divided, and anyway, babies were not petted for long. Velma quickly learned to "take back tit," as the rude saying went. By the time she was four, she had a younger brother to look after. By the time she was eight, she could cook a passable meal and clean house. By the time she was ten, she was doing field work. She used to joke at our supper table that her favorite pieces of chicken were the gizzard and the tail. All her life her feet bore the marks of the too-tight, hand-me-down shoes she wore as a schoolgirl, just as her mind bore the marks of the one-room schoolhouse at Buckville, Arkansas.

And yet her childhood was joyous, not grim. She'd finish her work and burst out of the house to roam the woods with her brother Cecil and their good dog Ranger. She learned to climb trees and fight. She never combed her hair. She was star forward on the Buckville basketball team — the girls played by boys' rules — and she was an excellent sprinter. She may sound like one of those ingratiating little Southern tomboys out of Carson McCullers or Harper Lee, but no one thought of her as a tomboy. She was merely a wild little girl. Her passage to adulthood was easy; she was a grown woman by the time she was fourteen, a square-cut beauty with brown curls (she took up combing eventually), green eyes, wide shoulders, big hands. I have snapshots of her in flounced dresses (she copied newspaper patterns) and flapperish pumps and little felt hats. Her generation was the first in the farming South to look toward town, to break the terrible old rule of utter self-sufficiency, to dare to cross the bridge into civilization. She and her sister were the first of their line to buy readymade dresses or hear a radio or have electric lights or drive an automobile. Even their parents began to want *things*. One day in 1925 their father astounded the chickens and mules and his kids by bouncing up the rutted wagon trail in a Model T. That car was Mother's idea of liberation. It meant that she and her sister and their girlfriends and beaus could escape from the front porch.

Soon everybody had a car, or at least everybody who succeeded in courting Velma had one. My favorite photograph of her shows her at age fifteen, the summer of 1929, her dark hair bobbed and finger waved, her long, silky legs crossed as she perches on the front bumper of an outsized flivver with the headlights peering over her shoulders like the eyes of a stone god. Every young man in Garland County wanted to marry her, and the same year the picture was taken, she nearly lost her head: she went as far as the Justice of the Peace with one poor devil but changed her mind outside the door and made him drive her home.

Another event of that year was the stock market crash, of which she was certainly unaware, never having heard of the Stock Exchange and not being a reader of newspapers. Nevertheless, the Depression put a decisive end to any future she might have envisioned on some prosperous farm. Until the 1930s, the backwoods people had managed to tack into unfavorable economic winds by picking up and moving a hundred or so miles farther west to a new farm, but now there was no place to go but town, and no use hunkering down and hoping the storm would pass. This storm was clearly not going to pass over, not until the rural South had been almost obliterated.

In the 1930s the South had the highest birthrate in the nation, the greatest burden of excess humanity. Southerners had always looked upon their children as wealth — free labor, free entertainment, good company. Now this multitude was a national liability, the complicating factor in what Franklin Roosevelt called "our number one economic problem." People set out once more for parts unknown, but this time in cars, not wagons, and this time in search of jobs, not land. Millions of Southerners did as my mother did: they went to the nearest town. She was not at all sorry to go. She moved into a tumbledown house with her married half-sister and got a job as a maid cleaning tourist cabins at a salary of three dollars per week. I asked her once if she had liked the job, and she said, "No, but it sure beat picking peas."

At twenty she got married, not to any of her country suitors but to a city man, a Yankee from Indiana, who wouldn't allow salt pork in the house and liked his beef rare. (If he had expressed a preference for live rattlesnakes on his plate, my mother's brothers could hardly have been more disgusted.) His culinary preferences were irrelevant, anyway, because it was three years before he was able to buy groceries on a dependable basis. Before they were married, he had confessed to my mother that he was a bookmaker, which she took to mean bookbinder, and he encouraged her for a time in this fallacy. He was a strange choice for her, this articulate, luckless gambler who was in a double sense a man of books. Not that he talked of books to her. He took her driving in his brand-new Pontiac on moonlit nights and made her pose for snapshots outdoors — in the daylight — in a black teddy.

She never told me what she had seen in him, or what, as a young wife, she had expected him to provide for her. When I knew him, he was gray-haired and had grown fat, but something handsome still lingered in his face. I once found a snapshot of him at age twenty — a tall, thin, blond youth with a cutting nose and a reckless look. I always saw this image in him, rather than what he was. My mother must have, too, though by the time she emptied out that bedside drawer and foreswore loving him, the querulous, obese, and bitter man had obliterated the blond youth forever.

The glamour of him, the sheer exoticism, must have been the reason she married him. How strange he must have seemed to a farm girl newly arrived in town. The only thing he had in common with her kinfolks was his reliable lack of currency. He used to reminisce sometimes about how he married her without two dollars to pay the judge. The Pontiac got repossessed. Once when my mother was four months' pregnant, they had to go without food for three days. I was born on credit, even though the doctor's fee was only five dollars. This is the sort of glamour and exoticism that gets old fast. And if Velma had married to escape her heritage, she made a fatal mistake, for he hung her heritage around her neck like a bag of asafetida and mocked her for it, growled at her and all her relations for being unlettered simpletons, whom he trusted his daughter would not emulate. That, rather than any standard rivalry over my father's affections, was what dug the first ditch between her and me. (It dug a deeper one, later on, between him and me.)

I was always half Yankee, then and now. Sometimes more than half. I grew up zigzagging, as children do, between love and antagonism for my mother, who in my view had no existence prior to mine and had, in fact, been born of me. She was an excellent mother. Oh, how tired I got sometimes of her excellence, the cleanliness, the godliness, the puffed sleeves, the hundred strokes of the brush on my hair, Velma's darling in a pinafore, never late to school. By this time my father was working as a cashier in the casino and bringing home a paycheck every Saturday. Now they had a house of their own, where Mother spent her time scrubbing floors and keeping everything germ-free. Her energy was terrifying. She burned enough calories each day to run a hundred-acre farm, and in her imagination that was what she was doing — in a five-room frame house with only three occupants, where the only livestock was a puppy. Yet no matter how ferociously she applied soap powder to everything, she never became quite domesticated or dowdy. Her house never ate her up. She was like a master gardener suddenly put in charge of one flowerpot, and she did her tasks with the ease of a professional. I was always aware of the strength she had in reserve.

Children, presumably, are struck at an early age by the mysterious bond that exists between their mothers and fathers, but what my mother and father felt for each other seemed natural enough to me. I often wished the mystery were a little thicker, that they loved each other more. As I grew up, however, what was impenetrable to me was not their love but mother's love for her own mother. Between these two there was no generation gap, no chasm. My mother never racked her brains explaining why she and her mother couldn't relate. Lavisa Eugenia McElroy Loyd was Mama, and all her children felt the same fierce love for her. Far from dreading her visits — as so many women I know secretly do — my mother looked forward to being under the same roof with her mother. "Mama is coming to stay with us awhile," was a boast, not the presentiment of a nervous breakdown. When Mama did come into town, she had to take turns staying with all her children, else there would have been a family fight. And though it was an interminable, dusty voyage, my mother was always eager to go to her mama's house.

It was a long day's journey begun in darkness, and like the journeys undertaken by adventurous youths in fairy tales, it took us over many a hill and through many a thicket of briars. We would set off early on a day guaranteed by the weather forecast to be fair, for the final obstacle in our path was a swift river without any bridge. For days in advance my mother inquired "Is the North Fork up?" of any travelers from that direction. The current was quite powerful enough to upend our green Chevrolet coupe and to send us to rest face downward on the riverbed. We always got across, but I would hang my head out the window as far as I dared, hoping we wouldn't capsize, and the sight of water swallowing the running boards gave me the imagery for an eerie dream that has recurred all my life. I am a passenger in a car, sometimes the driver. As we speed along the road, I notice that the road is dissolving, but I cannot stop. The engine roars as we plunge slowly forward into a widening lake.

The house Grandma lived in was as wide as a mansion, unpainted pine, with a porch that ran along the front, where we children ran clattering up and down, for the planks were not tightly nailed. Through the middle of the house was a breezeway where Ranger spent his air-conditioned afternoons. Grandma always had a dog named Ranger, long after the original hound was gone. On one side of the breezeway were the kitchen and the "front room"; on the other, two vast bedrooms, each with four feather beds made up with rough linen and no counterpanes. On the front porch were a shallow enamel basin and a bucket and dipper and a bar of Cashmere Bouquet, which had recently replaced the homemade lye soap. We were forbidden to waste water — what we didn't drink out of the dipper we emptied into the basin for wash-ups. In the clean-swept front yard was an oak tree with its root system coiled above ground, and there we children set up housekeeping, sweeping each crevice with a pine-needle broom, building furniture from nutshells and bits of glass, borrowing spoons from the kitchen, fighting over whether to play school or house and who would get to be the mother.

On the porch, in the front room, in the redhot kitchen, women would be embracing, cooking, tasting, scouring. The men scattered out into the fields or under the trees, but the women, home for Sunday, filled the house. I never saw them so animated as when they were together that way, so open-handed. If any dark Freudian knots complicated my mother's feelings toward Lavisa Eugenia, she certainly buried them deep. If Freud had spent his time talking to my grandmother rather than Viennese ladies with hysterical paralysis, his psychoanalytical theories would have been very different.

When I was four, my grandma died. The funeral was a solemn event — the grief of two counties was roused. People came from all over, in cars, trucks, wagons, buggies. Some walked barefoot up the dirt road to the cemetery. I remember little about the crowd. Standing in a churchyard on a windy September day, under a sun still stoked up to its August fury, I stared at the brutally plain pine box and the hole in the ground where it was soon to be placed. The preacher began to pray and shout, reading long passages from the Scriptures. He worked the crowd like a wild-eyed musician pumping up an old pipe organ. Grown men began to sob aloud, and the smelling salts went from hand to hand. Several of the women had to be half carried away to a row of chairs in the shade. A ghastly old accordion, with no tune at all in its insides, began to wheeze, and the broken voices sang:

> *Father alone we'll know all about it.*
> *Father alone we'll understand why.*
> *Cheer up, my brother, live in the sunshine.*
> *We'll understand it all, by and by.*

I was speechless, dumbstruck with the knowledge that my mother, my father, and perhaps even little children are subject to being laid out in pine boxes. Moreover, my mother, after weeping into a handkerchief for most of the ceremony, lost control and sobbed and screamed and collapsed on the ground. I could hardly endure the sight of it. Not until years later did it occur to me that she was not quite twenty-five on the day of the funeral, an orphan. But I knew that her love for the woman lying there had in it something that tore the heart out, something I dreaded and did not wish to understand.

I loved my mother, too, but not that way. That love frightened me. Years later, when I encountered the word "atavistic," I knew immediately what it meant. From mother to daughter for a dozen generations, perhaps a hundred thousand, had come this unspoken counsel, this taciturn resolve to work until your skin turned to leather, and your back never stopped aching, to do the labor of ten men, if necessary, and to seek in your progeny your only real sense of accomplishment. For such women, their first and perhaps only allegiance was to their children. They would have died for them, like a grizzly bear in her tracks, in a devotion equally unreasoning. (This is by no means an exclusive Southern trait, but it had ample room to develop in the backwoods: it was what was written in the faces of those desperate sharecropper mothers in the 1930s photographs.)

I wanted no part of this. I wanted a pretty, well-dressed mother who kept her fingernails painted and wore a fur coat to P.T.A. meetings.

*   *   *

In a piece about Black English for the *New York Times*, James Baldwin observed that language is "the most vivid and crucial key to identity: it reveals the private identity and connects one with, or divorces one from the larger, public, or communal identity." My mother had such a language of identity — hillbilly English, which once was just such a key to identity as James Baldwin describes. The Southern migrant in the twentieth century has been forced to carry it around like a cardboard valise, evidence that he is a transient arriving in vain at the door of Grand Hotel. Hillbilly English was the language of the dying frontier, of the farm and the backwoods in an ancient social order. Not much is left of it now except in show business. It makes the Grand Ole Opry grand, and it was what made L'il Abner funny. In the movies it marks out the rubes and the demagogues, as it has in many novels, Faulkner's or James Dickey's *Deliverance*, for example. Its wiry, leathery locutions come with a mythic overlay thrown in for free — poor white trash, mean and lowdown. Ignorant. Dumb. Like Black English, it causes doors to be slammed shut. This was my mother's speech, and it separated us. Women have carved identities distinct from their mothers' by having lovers or going to law school or getting married at dawn in their bare feet, but my ticket to independence was standard English.

Folklorists, out in the high hollows with tape recorders, have been telling us for decades that the ancient speech habits of the Southern mountains date back to Renaissance English and have miraculously survived unscathed, just like the dulcimers that presumably hang on the wall of every cabin. They cite old forms like "holp" for "helped," "ary a one" for "none," and other archaisms dear to the hearts of grammarians. Dear to my heart, too, for I can remember hearing this language used in earnest. Even as late as the 1950s, hillbilly English was still in a fairly pristine state in backwoods Arkansas, and I'm as eager as anybody to give it an Elizabethan pedigree.

It was as rough as a fresh-sawed board, with none of the cadences of the Tidewater accent or the soft resonances of black speech. It twanged like an out-of-tune banjo, and if Shakespeare was its great-grandsire, its more immediate ancestry was ignorance, abetted by isolation. After she moved to town, my mother struggled daily not to say "I taken" and "he don't." She learned, after several years, that what you did to a shirt collar was not "arning" and what an automobile had four of was not "tars," and that "them" was not the same as "those." She left off saying she was "aimin' " to do a thing, but never got rid of "hisself" and "theirself." Alas, there were no linguists hanging around Hot Springs to reassure her that she sounded like a seventeenth-century English peasant.

How I shrank from it, as I had shrunk from my grandmother's coffin. But what a wonderful language it was. People didn't leave, they "taken off," and they takened off their clothes and takened a dose of salts. (I never figured out when to add the *ed* to it.) They never searched for a thing: they "hunted it up," and they did as they "ort." They "warshed" things out, and then they "rinched" them. My aunt Vera, of legendary tidiness, spent a lifetime rinching her hair, her underpants and her dishrags, rinching off her porch, her feet, or her nieces who had been making mudpies. She and my mother were forever "fixin' " to do this or that, and if you asked when, they always said, "dreckly," which is "directly," but meant "when I get around to it."

If they wanted a hug from a child they commanded, "Give me some sugar," and sassy kids were threatened with "little keen switches across them bare laigs." The *a* at the end of a given name was usually transformed into *y*. (Four sisters I knew whose names were Edna, Elva, Nola, and Lola, have gone through life as Edny, Elvy, Noly, and Loly. There was a fifth, but her name had been Roxy to start with.) In hillbilly, people never scolded anybody, they "quarreled at" a person, and anyone in a bad temper was "a-quarrelin' " — "Yonder comes my papa just a-quarrelin'," or "mad as an old sore-tailed cat."

People were seldom in love; they were "foolish about" somebody. "He's just foolish about Maria." Cheese and cabbage and molasses were spoken of in the plural. "Pass me those cheese," or " . . . them cheese." "Bed" was never just bed, but "the bed." Nobody went to bed, he "got in the bed," and lazy people "laid in the bed" until whatever late morning hour they got out of the bed.

It was a language generous with pronouns. Never "let's," but "let's us." "Let's us go on over to your allses house and eat us some dinner." "Hunt you up a rockin' chair, and set down awhile." This double-barreled, nailed-down dative was used whenever it possibly could be. People were always urging me to "put you a spoonful of them good preserves" on my biscuit, or "drink you a glass of that cold buttermilk." There was something tender and owlish in this odd locution, as if one ought to perform these homely acts with thankfulness that the benefit of them was strictly personal, something that did not need to be divided up and shared.

Hard workers were the "workingest," fast runners the "runningest," sagging barns the "torn-downest," smart dogs the "beatin'-est." Adjectives were generally frowned on, but you could always take the small plain ones and lay them on in threes — "a great big ole," "a tiny little bitty," "a hateful mean ole." It was as lavish and unstudied as country hospitality. The days of log rolling and corn husking were past by the time I was born, but the spirit was the same. People hardly ever issued specific invitations. The courtesy was not to invite but to go. People just showed up and were always made welcome: it was an excuse to stop work. To stay less than an hour was an insult, and there was always a meal. Nobody ever was let out of a house without the goodbye ritual, which could take up to three hours. "No, now you don't have no business going off so soon, you just got here." "Now, come on, stay all night with us, don't say no." And in working out the details of a refusal or acceptance, the talk would begin again. I have wasted away on many a doorstep while my mother spent the afternoon saying goodbye at some second cousin's home.

All this was topsy-turvy from uptown manners, just as the grammar was crazy. It drove me mad. By the age of ten I had become a snob, as fearful of dangling my participles as of laying hold of the wrong fork at some well-set dinner table. Nobody north of the Mason-Dixon line would have been able to see much difference between my mother's manners and those of our city friends, but she was definitely an outsider. Furthermore, she knew she embarrassed me. I knew I was being an ass, even then, and I tried not to be embarrassed. But it was not the surface of her speech that mattered — it was its connotations, the closemouthedness, the toughness, the weight of familial devotion it carried.

"A language," Baldwin said, "comes into existence by means of brutal necessity, and the rules of the language are dictated by what the language must convey." Hillbilly was all hardship and conspicuous self-denial and rough wit. No fancy words. Nothing abstract. It was a tool for hellfire sermons, bawdy jokes, gospel songs, and insults. In its very vocabulary was contempt for all things intellectual. But it was clean and sweet. It is as old as Black English and as great a liability. Mother spoke a pretty version of it, but I took care not to talk like "thet."

Between her and me there was much anguish. As any second-generation immigrant knows, to refuse to speak the language of one's ancestors is the ultimate breach. Yet she was able to forgive me one way or another for such tricks as going into the country with her and calling all the women "ahnt" instead of "aint."

* * *

As I have said, my mother was not an ideologue, nor given to analyzing things, and what she might have thought of the modern feminist movement I cannot say. Out on the farm the subject of women's rights was irrelevant, but she did come to believe in women's rights once she began working for wages. (In much the same way, she believed in Saint Peter waiting at the Pearly Gates. There had to be such a thing, even though she had never personally seen it.) Her job at the tourist cabins for three dollars a week was a fair enough beginning. She had many other kinds of work after that. Running a mangle in a laundry was one of the things she did before I was born. About the time my father decided to become a farmer, when I was thirteen, his health and fortunes began to fail. Mother went right back into the job market, selling clothing and shoes in various department stores, clerking and cashiering in a drugstore, taking in sewing on weekends. She both worked and kept house, and she nursed my father through diabetes and other ailments that finally carried him off.

The best job mother ever had was as assistant physical therapist in a local hospital that treated arthritis. She had had to train for the post, and it had a semblance of professional status even though it was hard labor, often in a steamy therapeutic pool. She liked it, though. It was the only job she had that didn't seem pointless. She began there in 1959 and by 1967 had worked up to sixty-five dollars a week. Men on the hospital staff doing exactly the same work made more, but there was no point protesting. The threat of a layoff was all too vivid. She could have been replaced the next day. Of all the Southern states only Texas ratified the Equal Rights Amendment (Tennessee and Kentucky ratified but rescinded), and one state, Mississippi, never even gave suffrage a *pro forma* Yea. Not surprisingly, Southern working women fare worse than any in the nation. "Blacks and women," according to a report of the Southern Regional Council, continued through the 1970s to hold low-status, low-paying jobs. In 1975, not one black woman was making as much as $13,000 per year, and in the sixteen Southern cities surveyed, only one per cent of all skilled workers were women. The Southern female, who is supposed to hold so special a niche in the fond masculine heart, has had rough treatment in the marketplace.

Not too surprisingly, therefore, Mother never perceived work as anything exciting or glamorous. It was something you did because you needed the money. You had no union, no seniority, and no guarantee that your responsibilities would not be increased by 50 per cent without any commensurate rise in salary. Benefits, of course, were something accruing to the employer. So whatever job she had, she took care to get to work early and stay late. When her supervisor, always a man, spoke harshly to her, she took her rebukes mildly and spoke her mind only at home. Her preference — and in this she was at one with most of the women she knew — would have been not ever to work for wages at all. Housework struck her as easy and satisfying by comparison. At least in the house she was in charge of something.

But in one way, Mother was a kind of radical, or at least events turned in such a way that she began to look like a radical. Some time in the late 1960s feminists brought forth the notion of sisterhood — of women bonded to women. Sisterhood was going to be "powerful," our Hanseatic League, our lobbying arm in the corridors of heightened awareness. But sisterhood was nothing new to me. It has been a zealously guarded secret among Southern women for years. Next to motherhood, sisterhood is what they value most, taking an endless pleasure in the daily, commonplace society of one another that they never experience in male company.

The most vivid memories of my childhood are long afternoons when my aunt Vera would come to our house with her daughter, June, and the four of us would form a kind of subversive cell. June and I would usually play, indoors and out, while our mothers sewed or quilted or canned. Sometimes the four of us would dress and get in the car and drive around Hot Springs, buying thread and snaps at the dry-goods store, visiting some spring or other and drinking from tin cups, or "ratting up and down," as my aunt called it, on Central Avenue. Hearing what they said on these afternoons, I gradually realized that my mother and her sister were not awed by men in the least, that they preferred each other's company to that of their respective husbands.

I also realized that these two women had certain unmatronly desires, usually involving beautiful dresses and travel, that otherwise went unmentioned: merely the circumspect fantasies of a pair of young housewives caught in the coils of the commonplace. And yet, sharing these fantasies made them laugh, gave them a secret life as they bent their dark heads over the sewing machine or a "pinker" that never would pink. I could not have voiced the idea, but I knew that the part of their lives they liked most was here, with each other. Not at the supper table or at work or in bed with their husbands. My father used to be jealous of these tête-à-têtes, and he had cause.

Often I spent summer afternoons in larger groups of women, not my kin. The neighborhood beauty shop is one of the foundations of society in small Southern towns. You go there to get your hair "fixed," but that isn't the real reason, any more than men congregate at the county courthouse to transact legal business. The beauty operator is invariably a middle-aged woman who found herself in need of a trade and solved the problem by getting her license and having some shampoo sinks and hair dryers installed on the glassed-in porch. All the neighborhood women would have standing appointments, as my mother did, and they'd bring their children along. It was an all-female society — no man would dare enter the place — and here, if nowhere else, women said what they thought about men. And what they thought was often fairly murderous.

Those sweet-faced wives and mothers would sit there wafting their wet, red fingernails in the air, hoping to get them dry before the comb-out was finished, saying, "Now, Maidie, spray me good, I want it to last through tomorrow. I'll sleep with my head in a bonnet." They would gossip, of course. Every teen-age romance or impending marriage, separation, illness, operation, or death got its going-over. But the leitmotif of the song they sang was their loyalty and fortitude in the face of male foolishness, and as a keen obligato, "Don't ever let them know what you really think of them. Humor them. Pretend you love them. Even love them, if you must. But play a strong card to their weak one." That was not what they said, but it was what they meant, and it is an attitude that often runs through the conversations and the writing of Southern women.

It was always the same, wherever I went. As they drank their cokes, folded their stacks of fresh towels, played bridge, or sewed, they assured one another, "Men are children. Men are little boys. They can't stand pain. They never grow up. They can't face the truth." All this information was deeply buried in metaphor. "Albert got up at three o'clock to go fishing this morning. Was just going to tiptoe out, he said. Well, he couldn't find his hipboots, and I thought he would tear the house down. I finally had to get up and find them for him. It was five by the time he left." Or, "I told him if he wanted to smoke that nasty pipe, he could smoke it outside. I wasn't going to have that smell in my living room." Or, "He's just like a little child. If you don't have supper on the table the minute he gets home, he gets mad. 'Course, after you feed him, you can get him to do anything."

This was their means to survival, a minority strategy worked out and handed along from mother to daughter. But it was a very hard bargain, hardest in some ways for the men. Southern men, and in particular the writers, are as a rule so fixated in their points of view that they seldom realize what the women are thinking about them — or doing to them. Occasionally, one of them suspects what is happening. James Dickey was quoted in the *New York Times* on the subject of Southern women. "They're very loving and affectionate, but they really think their men are dependent upon them. If their man is brilliant, they think he's brilliant because they've helped him to be brilliant. Basically they think their men are weak . . ."

Southern women are supposedly taught to bat their eyelids and be weak, but I know very few of them who are truly dependent, no matter what they may pretend. In the end, how can they have perfect respect for people they regard as small boys to be tolerated, put up with, cajoled? "If I ever finish my education, I'm going to live in the North," a young black woman said to me recently in Atlanta. "I told my daddy I was, and didn't he get mad! So then my mother scolded me, and she said, 'Don't you know that's no way to handle your daddy? If you want him to give you the money to go North, at least wait to ask him until after he's had a good meal, and then talk sweet to him. Don't just up and tell him what you are going to do.' That's always what Mother says. I went to visit my cousins in Brooklyn last summer, and they say what they think, whether anybody has had a good dinner or not."

* * *

My mother and I were double-sided people, often at cross-purposes. She felt her responsibilities toward me keenly and tried to make a woman of me (she must have despaired of the task, since I was indolent by nature and spent most of my time listening to radio serials and reading. What she taught was not necessarily what I learned. Her spoken lessons were just what any good mother of the 1940s was teaching her daughter. But what she really wanted me to know I learned by going to the movies and the beauty parlor with her and through what I overheard her saying to my aunt as they sewed. I listened well. I was a better student than she thought. But one of the things she most wanted me to learn was something I never quite absorbed: dissimulate. Hide. Never let anybody know what your true feelings are. Unlike that of the belle, however, her purpose was defensive rather than predatory.

Psychiatrists, understandably enough since most of them are men, have always focused on the passion that little girls feel for their fathers. Girls are all supposed to be in training from babyhood, sensing out the contours of love and loss as we fall in love with Daddy and are forced to postpone our pleasure. But I was in love with my mother, too. I hated her doing housework, could not bear the sight of her in an old dress and a pair of unlaced oxfords, feeding soapy bed sheets into the wringer, scraping carrots and parsnips at the sink. But one thing she had acquired in town was the ability to be glamorous, to divorce herself, by means of paints and polishes, from that other world. I loved her glamorous aspect.

She had a wonderful drawer full of cosmetics. I think the women in her family must have yearned for such things since the dawn of time. In any case, my mother thought that make up was one of the fine arts. She had an enormous dressing table, a yellow satin-veneer piece with a knee-hole and a mirrored top, and a vast standing mirror that reflected the whole bedroom. There was a little low-backed bench and four drawers; in them she kept all her wonderful implements of beauty. Not every day, but once a week, or any time she was going out shopping, she would bathe, put on her stockings and a lacy slip and high-heeled shoes, and sit down to paint. I would abandon dog, swing, book, or any other pursuit in order to watch her. I'd come indoors and post myself beside the bench.

The open drawers gave off the most ravishing smells. Down in their depths sat little white jars with pink lids, black cylinders trimmed in silver, pink glass things with tiny roses on top, high-domed boxes with face powder inside (if you opened these on your own, they'd blow dust all over the table top), fresh powder puffs, miniature caskets with trick openings, compacts with pearl lids that shut with a glamorous click, vials of astringent and witch hazel, red boxes with logs of mascara inside, and pencils for what Mother always called her "eyebrowls." Most seductive of all were the perfume bottles, some with glass stoppers and ribbons around the neck, one with a figurine on top. (No doubt there was enough coal-tar dye and other harrowing poisons in this array to have murdered any number of Renaissance popes. This was long before we learned to fear our own chemical magic. Maybe, in fact, the paint pots were what killed her.)

She would take her tweezers and hand mirror, search her freckled face for any wayward sprouts and swiftly uproot them. Anxious about a black hair or two on her upper lip, she would apply a thick paste, that looked like a pale green caterpillar beneath her nose. It had to set five minutes, and it had a loathsome vinegary stench. I smell it still. When she removed the goo, she looked exactly as she had before, but she would survey the defoliated terrain with the solemnity of a military tactician.

Meanwhile, I would be taking the tops off all the lipsticks and unscrewing jar lids, hoping to have a say-so in what she applied next. I liked the smoky eye shadow, the blue rouge (it *was* blue), the dark maroon lipstick, and whatever came in exotic packaging. But she seldom followed my leads, except on the evenings she went out alone. My parents never went out together, but once every few weeks or so, after doing the supper dishes, Mother would dress and disappear and neither she nor Daddy would tell me where she was going. I imagined her meeting handsome men, sipping coffee with them in the grill room of some hotel. It turned out, years later, that what she did was go to the movies by herself, while I agonized at home, pleased by the notion that she was having a romance and ravaged with jealousy at the same time — jealous of what, I still can't say.

On those rare afternoons when she did abandon her housework and go out, she would leave the blue rouge and maroon lipstick in their cases, and having brought her face to its state of daytime perfection, she would take up her car keys and shut the door on her immaculate house. She and I would set off for town together, and she seemed so beautiful to me in those moments that I loved her with all my heart — indeed I was in love with her. Unless we were going to the movies, town was a complete bust. We'd go find a parking place and go into Woolworth's for a spool of thread and a nickel's worth of candy. Maybe we'd look at a pattern book, and sometimes, to my despair, she'd bump into one of her thousands of cousins on the street and talk for half an hour. The exoticism of the afternoon would vanish sooner than the bag of candy.

Many years later I stopped to wonder why a woman of her thoroughly practical inclinations would spend upwards of an hour prettying up to go to the dime store. She certainly was not trying to attract a man. In the middle of the afternoon in Hot Springs, Arkansas, the only visible men were pumping gas in filling stations. She was not doing it for Daddy, for by the time he got home from work, she'd be in a housedress again, perspiring over the kitchen range. Nor was she competing with other women. She was doing it for fun, and for a mark of her separateness, and for a way of showing herself — and me — that even so responsible a person as herself could do something that had no purpose to it. It was her one real break with her past. Maybe she wanted to let me know, in the most subtle way, that femininity was not merely the massive, serious, strenuous thing she usually made it seem to be, but occasionally a matter of pleasing yourself. And thus she delved into that dresser drawer, which is one of the most ancient sources of womanly corruption, without being corrupted by it.

One August morning, when I was thirty-three and a long-gone Northerner, I stood beside Mother at the very same dresser drawer and once again watched her make up her face. Her right hand was faltering that day; for a reason that she claimed not to understand her fingers could not quite handle the stoppers and lids and paraphernalia. Once again, I helped a bit, undid the caps, snapped the little containers shut. I knew, although she did not quite yet realize it, that she was dying. The mastectomy four years earlier had not cured the cancer, which had instead metastasized into a clump of wild cells now thriving in the left lobe of her brain, and in her spine, her ribs, her femurs, her tibias. Nevertheless, on this morning she had awakened optimistic, feeling better, she said. She wanted to get dressed and go out. Worn out by the effort, she lay down, and in the afternoon she had the first of several seizures — an intimation of mortality, a fast and vicious dress rehearsal for her death throes six months later. Then I think she realized what was wrong, though she did not say so, even after the terror had let up. After that day, there was no more frivolity. She never opened the dresser drawer again.

* * *

The South may be the last place where dying is still sometimes a community project. My father died two years before my mother, but his stay in the hospital, as the obituaries say, was brief. Mother's illness, which went on for six months, reached out and transformed the daily routine of a dozen people. Sometimes, sitting at her bedside and knowing exactly who would arrive and at what time, I used to wonder what we all had done before she got sick. I had left my husband and my job in New York and had come to stay with her full time. I could have hired a nurse, I suppose, to stay with her at home, during the few weeks she was well enough to be at home. But the indecent passion she had felt for her mother at last laid hold of me. I couldn't bear the idea of anyone but me waiting on her, cutting up her food in tiny pieces, washing her nightgowns, cleaning her house, taking her a bedpan at 3 A.M. Exhausted at one point, I considered hiring a nurse or a housekeeper but the whole family recoiled. It had to be my hands and their hands. It was the only way we could confront our rage at what had overtaken her.

As her spine dissolved, and her speech worsened, and she lost the ability to read and write, and she became almost immobile, I took a certain grim pleasure in making her as comfortable as I could. She was doing what she could for me, too. She seldom cried out, and she never complained, even though a change of sheets or merely having the bed cranked up was almost unbearable agony. She used to pretend to be asleep every afternoon so I could read, and I read the way a chainsmoker smokes — getting through two or three paperbacks a day, piling the used-up novels on the dresser, by the chair, in the corner of the room, like unemptied ashtrays.

She finally went to the hospital so that she could have injections of morphine. (Ironically, she almost always refused them. She said they didn't kill the pain but locked her up inside it.) This was a homey, almost countrified place where the needs of the dying were understood and always had been. The nurses brought me a cot so I could spend the nights, and for almost six months I lived there with her. In order to keep ourselves intact, she and I set up an unvarying routine: we awakened at seven as the morning prayer was broadcast over the loudspeaker. I gave her water and brushed her teeth. I brought the bedpan. Her breakfast came. I helped her deal with it. Then I changed her linen and got dressed myself and went outside in search of coffee. By then it would be eight o'clock, and I would go and telephone her sister and her brothers and her best friends, all of whom wanted a morning report regardless of the fact that they came to visit every afternoon.

That got us through to half past eight. I was always stunned by the hundreds of actions one could perform in a hospital room and still use up only ninety minutes of one day. The rest of the day proceeded just the same deliberate way, each hour measured out carefully, marked by arrivals and departures. She never wanted to talk about what was happening to her; the word "cancer" was not in her vocabulary. I felt, uneasily, that we ought to be talking about it. It was well enough, I guessed, to have hidden all the facts of love in this impenetrable caul of reticence all one's life, but we were grown women now, and she was dying. Could we not even talk of that? Yet neither of us ever spoke. And once again, as I think back on it, it scarcely matters. What could we have said?

At first her self-control was hard-won: her face often had a desperate look about it, and she would weep and then stop weeping without offering any explanation. But then she got control again, and the control eventually turned into serenity. Only once, in the final months, did I see it break. She awoke one morning in November and asked what date it was. It happened to be my birthday, and for reasons that I did not immediately understand, she began to cry. "Don't worry, Mother," I kept saying. "I don't care if it's my birthday. You don't have to give me a present." I dared not tell her she didn't have to bake a cake. "Tell you what, I'll go get some cupcakes, and we'll celebrate this afternoon."

That only made things worse, and then it dawned on me. Long ago she had made the revolutionary decision to have only one child, or at least not to have twelve children and then turn them into farmhands. So as she lay on her deathbed, the event mattered to her. She was, not crying because it was my birthday. She was crying because years before, on that same morning, she had been twenty-one and had had a baby. Now, in so short a time, a bewildered young woman stood beside her hoping to distract her from thoughts of death. I had assumed, as always, that her concern was for me. But she was grieving for another young woman.

In the last month of her life, she lost the power of speech almost completely: that hillside in the brain's left hemisphere where words are manufactured had apparently been eaten up, strip mined. Sometimes, with enormous effort, she could repeat a word or two if she watched my mouth very carefully. Sometimes, bending over her, I would call her Mama, and she would say the word. I could tell by the vexation in her eyes that she knew it was the wrong name for me, but it was all she could do. I'd always laugh, and she liked that. One evening her brothers and I were sitting around the hospital room, too tired to talk or think, just watching her sleep, all of us worn down with knowing that she was locked up in pain that might last for months more. She woke and saw us and moved her left hand, clearly in need of something. Her younger brother bounded up to do the guesswork — water? and injection? ice cream? No, she smiled, but we could see her growing impatient. Finally, when we had all tried everthing, she made an enormous effort. Like a kid who knows the answer to a riddle, she opened her mouth and said one clear syllable: "Brush." And so her brother brushed her hair, and she fell asleep again, and next day died.

I don't know how many women like her are still left. I don't know whether her doctrine is the right one — if that is the word to apply to her beliefs. She would have understood the things that many women are now determined to gain — titles, power, high salaries, the right to define themselves by male standards of success. She certainly knew firsthand why women need an education and good salaries, and it never occurred to her that they needed to apologize for working outside the home, or in it either.

But the idea that happiness is likely to result from having a succession of lovers she would have thought silly. To exchange the certainties of the kitchen and the laundry room for the risky pleasures of the boudoir would have struck her as a dubious bargain. She didn't believe that feminine liberation had anything to do with sex but rather with paychecks.

Nor could she ever have agreed that housework is degrading drudgery that ought to be sloughed off on the maid, or that children drag a woman down. In fact, the whole notion that an assiduous fussing over one's own self, an endless vigil over one's own feelings and moods, an elaborate absorption in one's own body could be a source of satisfaction or a way of life would have astounded her. I think she would have gotten a good laugh over the recent discovery of certain avant-garde women that the experience of having a baby and raising it is, after all, worthwhile. But she wouldn't have laughed too hard. She never was the sort to downgrade other people's accomplishments.

She was one of the mass of women who work as housewives or as underpaid help in the outside world. Urban, educated feminists tend to dislike them for being regressive and reactionary and a passel of ingrates. I myself have become some sort of urban, educated feminist, and my mother and I are still at crosspurposes. Particularly since my daughters were born, she has whispered in my ear each night as I slept, trying to remake me in her image. I battle her off as well as I can, but she touches me still, and I love her. I would not want my children to grow up without knowing what their grandmother thought.

Eight

Why Southern Women Leave Home

I have left the South twice in my life. The first time was against my will. When I was nine, my father decided that we had to move to California. He had somehow managed, long distance, to get himself a job as a machinist at the Navy dry dock on North Island in San Diego Bay. (Though I knew he could have dealt a dice table at Las Vegas, this was the first I had heard that he could handle battleship engines.) His essential homelessness had laid hold of him as it periodically did. He was sick of figuring bets in the casino, sick of Arkansas and the interminable Southern depression that had barely lifted even in the biggest of all wartime booms. He was determined to transplant us.

So one August, sweating like horses in our new wool traveling suits, we got on the train in Hot Springs station, with a number of trunks and suitcases, for the short run to Little Rock. There we made connections with the Choctaw Rocket, the Santa Fe's crack passenger train. Daddy knew the name of every class A train in the country and had promised me rides on all of them from the Twentieth Century Limited to the City of San Francisco. However, the Choctaw Rocket turned out to be the first and the last, for in six months we were back home. My mother and I were not transplantable.

The months in San Diego I recall in the same way I remember the bout of scarlet fever I had had a year earlier — pain and delirium mixed with boredom. In that easy port city of no discernible seasons or traditions, a tepid harbor accustomed to the ways of soldiers and sailors and the rootless and the drifting, we wore the mark of our origins too clearly. We set off every antibody in the local immune system. I might as well have been Daisy Mae Yokum from Smackover. In San Diego, I realized for the first time that some people didn't think Southerners were human. In *Sophie's Choice*, William Styron, as an emigré from North Carolina, describes how he evoked a similar reaction from Sophie's Brooklyn lover, who took him for a racist. But these Californians were just ordinary folks hating Southerners for the sport of it, back in the days before anybody cared what whites were doing to blacks.

Southerners were Arkies, Okies, clay eaters, hicks, tramps —creatures straight out of *Grapes of Wrath* and *God's Little Acre*, novels accursed under my father's roof, though at that moment he had none. To the tearful astonishment of my mother, landladies refused to rent to us. "Don't want any cracker folks around here," one said, and others shut the door as soon as we opened our mouths. Housing was scarce enough, even for people from Boston. It took us weeks to find a place to live. I set off to the local school, expecting that within a week or so I'd have installed myself, as usual, as teacher's pet. But they treated me like a yokel. Contemptuous of my hair ribbons and scrupulously ironed puffed sleeves, the principal actually checked me for head lice. A little boy asked me if I had hookworm. Were those my first pair of shoes?

Back in Arkansas in this epoch teachers harbored flat board paddles in their desks and practiced corporal punishment with grim delight. Nobody had ever hit me, but I had watched little boys undergo brutal whackings. The beatings, of course, made outlaws out of the mischievous children and prigs out of people like me, but in any case I took school very seriously and did not want to weave baskets or make pots. The California schools then were in some sort of proto-counterculture or hippie phase. Fourth grade spent most of the day doing crafts. I wanted to do long division, but these breezy young teachers wouldn't even give us homework, let alone grades. I began to put on airs and make supercilious remarks about the lack of report cards. While my classmates wove rush mats, I'd do sums or disassemble my Mickey Mouse watch.

Needless to say, I had no friends. One tropical January afternoon, to my surprise, a little girl invited me to come climb the fig trees in back of her house, two or three blocks from ours. I stayed until sunset, for the fig trees and the companionship were sweet. I thought I might like California. But then I asked permission to go indoors to the bathroom. My friend led me toward the kitchen window and called to her mother. A pink face with black curls blossoming all around it, like a bisque doll, leaned out through the fluttering curtains. Later I persistently remembered a satin bow tied under the chin but that is sheer malice. "Mommy," said my playmate, "this is the kid from Arkansas. Can she come in and use the toilet?" I went indoors. Inside the facility, as I began to wash my hands, I heard a commotion in the kitchen, and the mother's voice floated through the bathroom door: "How dare you bring that little hillbilly in here to dirty up my nice bath?" As I stood thoughtfully drying my hands, I noticed that I had made black hand prints all over the guest towel. I fled without saying goodbye, although any self-respecting hillbilly would have gone in the kitchen and beat the lady up.

Not long after that we went home. Mother had broken out in hives, and I was wan from nightmares. But California was not a wholly destructive experience. It taught me that, for some reason I had never before suspected, the South was alien, and you paid a price for coming from it.

Everybody must learn this lesson somewhere — that it costs something to be what you are. I concluded that being a hillbilly was better than having no identifiable origins at all. Back on my home ground, however, taking some kind of long-range, baleful revenge against those Californians, I became a blind Southern chauvinist, beyond the wildest hopes of my father. This was when I began mainlining Margaret Mitchell, and I read volume upon volume of other partisan stuff, local colorists by the peck. The public library stocked mostly historical novels, and I read enough of these to have induced irreversible coma in a more mature brain. I even sent off to an out-of-print book supplier for Thomas Dixon's unutterable old screed, *The Clansman*, about the brave knights of the KKK. I nodded sagely as he spoke of preserving civilization in the face of the Black Menace. Ah, the Lost Cause. My head reeled with clanking swords, passionate planters, beautiful barren brides who finally managed to produce an heir to the fine old name, French kisses under Spanish moss, duels, cavalry officers, the works.

Many years and a hundred novels later, I came upon a passage in *Madame Bovary* describing the education of the heroine at a convent in mid-nineteenth-century France. The nuns carefully shielded the young ladies from any solid fact and poured on the gooey elixir of religious sentimentality. Saints, candles, heavenly bridegrooms, pious renunciations, swoonings, tears. Emma lapped it up. Flaubert clearly knew every detail of it and understood in his merciless way that adolescent women, like rhinoceroses, adore cooling their tender skins in emotionally comfortable mudholes, but that unlike rhinoceroses, they may one day be required to stand up and walk out.

Sometime, probably in my early teens, I began dimly to grasp that the glorious Southland was not what I had taken it to be. Worse than that, I was not what I had taken myself to be. I had no moment of blinding revelation. I was like an idiot trying to learn chess: each new discovery puzzled me. I do recall one autumn afternoon when I stood among

the thin ranks of boosters lining Central Avenue to watch
the Hot Springs High homecoming parade. Here came the
marching band, all done up in black and gold, stepping
smartly and playing off key as usual, followed by several
convertiblefuls of princesses and queens. My girlfriends
sighed with envy, but I could not manage the sigh of envy.
It was a replay of my one-on-one bout with salvation in the
Baptist church. I wanted to have the right feelings, but I
couldn't. And then — how had they got invited? — came the
marching band from Langston High, where the black kids
went to school. They also played football, though not with
us. Their band stepped smartly, too, and also sounded sour,
which was perhaps pardonable since some of the marchers
had no instruments. None of them had uniforms. They
marched along in their old clothes.

Right there on the sidewalk my regional identity started
to unravel. In spite of my years of rigorous training at the
hands of Miss Mitchell and Mr. Dixon and the rest, I could
see I wasn't turning out right. Or else the South wasn't
turning out right. I began desperately trying to figure out
which. The conclusion I finally reached — ambiguous as it
was — drove me out of my homeland forever.

* * *

There is a whole subdivision of sociology that has devoted
itself to proving that Southern society is as caste ridden as
that of the Hindu, rigidly stratified by economics and by
color. John Dollard's *Caste and Class in a Southern Town*, a
famous work of the 1930s that is still in print, argued the
point persuasively. And certainly the news, in the 1960s, of
the murders of civil rights workers in Mississippi, of the
bombings of black churches in Birmingham, of riots in
Selma and recalcitrance in Prince Edward Country, Virginia, seemed to confirm what men like Dollard had said.
Ironically, what the sociologists believed about the inviol-
ability of the color bar was exactly what the militant seg-
regationists wanted the outside world to believe.

But where I grew up, in darkest Arkansas, things were

not ordered so neatly. There was a kind of caste system. There was segregation and a color bar. No black had the slightest hope of getting a decent education or becoming a professional. Yet such things were out of the question for most whites, too. Most of us were uniformly poor, regardless of race or creed, and tried to get along with one another without making up too many theories. It was a racist system but far less systematic than outsiders supposed.

In my own family we never used any kind of racist vocabulary. My mother would not have allowed it. According to her, pretty was as pretty did. Nobody was superior. Well, perhaps people who obeyed the law were superior to criminals, but I never heard her assert that white people as a group had any cause to feel superior to blacks.

In some situations, there was racial mixing. Hospitals, for example, hired both blacks and whites as lower-echelon help. They ate in the same dining room, and when they passed on the street, they stopped to chat, right out in the open. From our side of the fence it all seemed peaceful and right. We never stopped to think how it looked from the other side.

And yet it was all a hoax, a delicate scrim that hid — at least from me — what was really happening on the stage. In 1954, after segregated schools were declared unconstitutional, the harsh undercurrents of white supremacist thinking — hidden for so long under good manners and intellectual laziness and the unwillingness of both races to confront the truth — surfaced with terrifying force. Neighbors of ours, even relatives, kindly people I had known all my life, began to air their ugly feelings, taking it for granted that we would be of the same mind. Friends who used to drop by on a Sunday to talk fishing and politics now spent the afternoon on hot talk about integration

Acts of bloodshed were apparently in store. Any observations of mine to the contrary were quickly shushed up by my parents. Where, I wondered, had all these bigots and sadists come from — so many, so angry? Raised from childhood on my mother's ideas of decency and common courtesy and my father's partisanship for the losing side, I had naturally concluded that integration of the schools was a fine idea, a splendid idea — high time for it. Why didn't everybody agree with me?

But alas, I can hardly claim that civil rights was the issue uppermost in my mind. Another, far stronger sense of dislocation began to overwhelm me. The closer I got to becoming a grown woman, the more inhospitable my homeland looked to me. Never having been picked as homecoming queen, I became class valedictorian, and then I went to spend four years in a women's college in east Texas, which proved to be an excellent place to contemplate the Southern feminine mystique.

East Texas, and my college in particular, were on the cusp between the West and the South. About half the students were Southerners from Louisiana and Arkansas and Mississippi, as well as the farm country of east Texas (with a few city girls from Houston and Dallas mixed in), but the rest were Texans from the high plains, and they were noticeably different from the rest of us. They were a wilder, stronger breed: beside them we Southerners looked positively dainty. They were unfeminized. They had no interest in clothes, wore their hair cropped, slept late on Sunday mornings while we were putting on our pretty little hats and waiting for the bus to go to Sunday school. (Southern Baptists go to Sunday school, or can go, from babyhood to old age.) They all played golf and tennis, fenced like masters, and had won their life-saving badges, apparently, while still in grammar school. I was frightened to death of them, but I envied them, too, because along with their life-saving badges, they seemed to have earned some magic exemption from the fate the college clearly had in mind for most of us: it wanted to turn us Southern girls into Southern ladies.

Unlike Sweet Briar or Randolph Macon and most other Southern women's colleges, Texas State College for Women had never been a female seminary or finishing school for upper-class girls. It had begun in 1903 as an industrial arts school whose mission was teaching the daughters of the poor to earn a living. When I was there, the architecture was traditional red-brick Georgian, and there was a decent liberal arts overlay to the vocational courses. But though there had never been anything remotely aristocratic about it, it was run on the Southern pattern. Gracious living was our motto and our goal. We were forbidden to be seen outdoors in blue jeans or to smoke in dormitory living rooms or other locations "where gentlemen were likely to call," in the hopeful phrase of the student handbook. Not even seniors were permitted to stay out after one, and any student who drank so much as a glass of beer could be expelled. If we had been the virginal daughters of the finest families in antebellum Savannah, our morals could hardly have been the object of more solicitude.

Yet, in fact, we were almost all first-generation college students, the daughters of farmers, white collar workers, and merchants who had sent us to this place because the tuition was cheap and the curriculum practical. Hardly one of us stood any chance of becoming a lady, but all except the most rebellious among us submissively studied the ladylike arts in anticipation of what the Dean of Women told us was "woman's only true career," marriage and motherhood. I could not help noting that the Dean of Women herself and most of the faculty were single. In any case, learning to pour tea and refraining from smoking in the living room and obeying the myriad puritanical rules that the college had devised for us did not appear to me to have much connection with marriage and motherhood.

Nor did the beauty contests. I could not understand at the time why a women's college would have beauty contests, but there they were, eight or nine of them each year. This was all part of our training, as if we were some kind of bush-league boot camp for the Miss America Pageant. We were the sister college of Texas A & M, at a safe distance of two hundred miles, and we elected several "maids," from among whom the Aggie Corps Captains selected a Sweetheart. (She had to go to all the Aggie games and stand

and holler. It was against the rules for anybody, including spectators, to sit down while the team was on the field.) That was our first job each year. Then we chose a beauty from each class and an all school beauty. The winners were announced in a special assembly, and they all had full-page pictures in the yearbook, in formals and elbow-length white gloves. We also elected a Cotton Queen and her court, and a Posture Queen, whose uptilted bosom and under-tucked buttocks were to be our physical ideal. One year we even chose a Black-eyed Pea Queen, but what her function in life was I never discovered

The best part was the Redbud Pageant, which revolved around an elected Queen and an enormous entourage of princesses, each of whom curtseyed at center stage in a cloud of pastel net as her name was uttered into a microphone —"Princess Betsy of the house of Allen" and so on — until after a weary couple of hours the end of the alphabet had been reached. Outside the administration building stood a massive statue of a pioneer woman, a strapping old party in a sunbonnet and L'il Abner shoes who was supposed to represent the spirit of the school. I often wondered why she didn't lumber across campus and burst into the Redbud Festival like Don Juan's Stone Guest, confounding all the princesses and sending the Dean of Women to hell through a trapdoor. What on earth were these rehearsals for? Obviously the final triumph for all us Princess So-and-So's was to be the wedding march. White gloves and tulle for the very last time.

I was growing increasingly pessimistic about my chances of finding a place for myself in Southern life. Outside the walls, the crisis over public school integration was building ominously. Inside, as though none of it applied to us, we maidens were industriously preparing for our futures. I was, of course, going to be a teacher, like all good girls in those days — the perfect career for a wife who might want to work, just to help her husband out, but who would certainly not want to be out of the home when her children were there.

I had no aptitude for teaching, but it sounded better than being a nurse or an occupational therapist or a nutritionist or any other possibilities offered. I spent a whole semester devising a set of lesson plans on *Macbeth*, which I was supposed to foist off on a hypothetical roomful of students as a work relevant to their daily concerns. I could not see what *Macbeth* had to do with anybody's daily life, unless we all intended to become assassins, and I could not imagine perpetrating such a fraud. That surely couldn't be steady work.

Worse than that, unlike most young women my age I was lacking not only in suitors but also in any desire to marry. I trembled when the Dean of Women spoke of this sacred mission. I didn't want a sacred mission. Oh, maybe someday, as long as it wasn't too sacred and didn't entail "helping out" by teaching *Macbeth* as if it were Hints from Heloise. None of these thoughts, of course, would be so great a solecism now as then. And even then I might have gotten away with it had I not been so intent on making an issue of it. As Scarlett's Mammy was in the habit of saying, Southern girls of nineteen who are in need of husbands are not expected to make an issue of anything. They are supposed to be sweet-natured and tactful and to remind themselves that more flies can be caught with honey than with buttermilk.

Somehow my once-comfortable environment had been sucked through a black hole and turned into a foreign land. My immune system was working overtime again. One stifling afternoon during summer vacation before my senior year, I announced my various disinclinations to my closest relatives. My mother, my cousin June, my aunt Vera, and I still functioned as the solid bloc we had been since my childhood. June was now married and had a daughter, whom we loved all the more because she was a girl and could fit right into this proto-feminist cell of ours, this oasis where no man was admitted and where male foibles were often under examination.

We were, on this particular afternoon, at my cousin's house. The baby was napping, and since the only electric fan had been set up to blow in the direction of her crib, we made ourselves tall glasses of iced tea and sat in the back-yard shade. The temperature was 105, which was nothing unusual, and the ice in the tea had melted before we got out the back door. My mother collected the laundry from the clothesline and began to fold it, pouring sweat. The grass had grown ankle high overnight and made my feet itch. There were some chiggers, too, which raised vicious little welts on my legs. A desolate boredom, more frightening than the Sahara, illimitable as the Empty Quarter of Arabia, came over me. I was sick of all this. I did not wish to be next in line to supply an heiress for this society and a back yard for it to meet in. I wanted out — of everything, per-manently. I burst out saying so, in words that I cannot re-call but which had the effect of nitroglycerine.

A loud and angry discussion followed, and we all began weeping. My mother wept first out of fright. What would become of me? My cousin took her part, as always, for by temperament they were more truly mother and child than Mother and I were. My aunt tried, as usual, to defend me, for like me she was a malcontent, and we often made com-mon cause. But the best she could muster was a prediction that I would come around to another way of thinking. She was right, though on that dreadful day none of us had much expectation of it. In a rage, and on the verge of heatstroke, I began to cry, too. I knew that the only solution was to leave them — these women I loved in my body and bones — and seek my people in another country. And so one day the next spring, I did. After writing my last final exam, I packed up and headed out on a round-trip plane ticket, the other half of which I promptly cashed in as soon as I got to New York,

I did not know it, but I was part of a vast northward exodus. "I ain't good-lookin', and I doan dress fine, but I'm a travelin' woman with a travelin' mind," sang Bessie Smith many years ago, with portents both spiritual and sexual. Every year — and long before Bessie — the South has pro-duced its small quota of travelin' women who dread the high cost of living and dying in Dixie and find they have to depart. Like many other Southern phenomena, the northward exodus has a past, rooted back in the hard earth and with special meanings for women.

* * *

The Southern states have always been a kind of colony — not overseas, but at the interior of the United States. Ever since the eighteenth century, the Southern pattern has been cheap labor and raw materials — sugar, rice, cotton, and in our own time coal, soybeans, poultry, minerals, textiles — things to be loaded into trucks and sent north, where they are turned into wealth for other people. Even as the South has transformed itself over the past twenty years into something like an industrial power, the Southern economic machine has remained primarily "extractive," in the word of Professor Charles P. Roland, who studied the contemporary South in *The Improbable Era.* In the 1970s, he writes, "regional industry was still characterized by relatively low margins of profit, low payrolls, and low capital investment." And that colonial factor has persisted in other ways. Southern industry, for example, is still largely owned by outside stockholders and investors. Like any colonial economy the South has had one perennially reliable export commodity in addition to its raw materials — people. From the mid-1930s until about 1965, though the national population surged upward, every Southern state except Texas and Florida steadily lost population. The result has been a demographic shake-up that has in one way or another affected almost every American city and citizen, a kind of leavening of the land with a Southern yeast.

Most of this exodus came about in the massive overhaul of Southern agriculture that began to take place after World War II. King Cotton went elsewhere: west Texas and California raise more cotton now than any deep South state. During the 1940s alone, two million blacks, most of them farm laborers, went northward. In the space of one generation states like Mississippi, where two-thirds of the population had lived on farms before World War II, were turned upside down. By 1970, only one Mississippian in ten lived on a farm. (This did not mean that the farms were gone. In fact, the size of the average farm quadrupled, and agriculture output increased ninefold.). Now that this agricultural revolution has been accomplished, the outflow of Southerners has tapered off in the last decade and begun to be offset by immigration from the North.

By no means all the Southern evacuees were hillbillies, farm laborers, and displaced coal miners. The forces that worked against the poor, oddly enough, also worked against the young and the educated. College graduates as well as tenant farmers had trouble finding work in the South. And it was not only a question of finding work. In every graduating class, there were always one or two or three students who discovered, even as they accepted their diplomas, that a liberal education had somehow rendered them unfit for Southern life. In *North Toward Home,* Willie Morris of Yazoo City, Mississippi, drew his own portrait as a rising man of letters, a young intellectual of the 1950s repelled by the mindlessness of the average Southern male and the asininity of fraternity life at the University of Texas. One night as he surveyed the city of Austin from a hillside where he had been abandoned stark naked by his playful fraternity brothers, he had a flash of anger: " 'I'm better than this sorry place,' I said to myself, and be damned if I didn't believe it.' " Southern women, too, have come to that same furious conclusion, though for somewhat different reasons and usually not stark naked on a mountainside. Educated women, black or white, sometimes find the South not only temperamentally incompatible but downright hostile. The supply of female intellectuals, however skimpy the numbers may be, has always exceeded the demand.

I know perhaps a score of women who have fled for philosophical or emotional reasons rather than purely economic ones. White women as well as black have run away from the old segregated South, not wishing to participate in — or be victimized by — a system that operated largely for the financial benefit of white men. But they run away, too, from the ramshackle mythology of ladies and belles, virtuous Christian motherhood, and all the rest of it, sometimes in loathing but as often as not with a touch of regret for their own failure to measure up. By no means do all *bright* Southern women give up; some of the smartest and most serious of them stay in the South and manage to fit in, a source of puzzlement to those who cannot. The transplants I know come in a variety of shapes and sizes. Some have made successful, even distinguished, careers for themselves in the North, have married and had children. Some have done none of these things. And yet, when they explain why they left home, a certain leitmotif emerges: "I never was much of a success with boys. I'm tall enough to look 'em right in the eye, and I always did. Southern men, oh well, you know, they are always just a little simple-minded. You have to be flirtatious." The speaker is a rangy, affable redhead of perhaps forty who earns $30,000 a year as an executive in a New York public relations firm. She has invited me to lunch so we can talk about the South. "Good ole boys bore me. I never had any ambition to spend my life picking up after one of them, and I have to admit that not one of them ever wanted me to do it, either. In my home town — that's Yazoo City, Mississippi, the same as Willie Morris — the only reason a girl was sent off to college was that she wasn't engaged when she got out of high school."

At a wedding reception I meet a pleasant woman, perhaps sixty and with just enough Southern accent to give away her origins in the Long Island suburb where she lives: "I was always very plain. You can see that for yourself. But my younger sister was a belle. If I had stayed in the little Tennessee town where I was born, I'm sure I'd never have married. I was type-cast as an old maid by the time I was ten. So after I finished school, I headed for Greenwich Village." She shows me photographs of her grown-up daughters, one an actress, the other a pianist. "I'm hardly a nonconformist," their mother adds. "I don't even believe in women's liberation. All I ever wanted, really, was my husband and family. But they make it too hard on their ugly ducklings down there, particularly the ones that never turn into swans."

"I always loved the stock market and I wanted to be an editor and writer on a big financial magazine," says an elegant ex-Southerner of perhaps thirty-five. "Now, how could I have done a thing like that in North Carolina? I'll tell you something, though. It's a help to be a Southern girl in the all-male world I work in. Northerners like sweet-talk and good manners, too. It tickles 'em to think I have a brain besides."

"I'm gay, you know," another journalist tells me, this one perhaps ten years younger than the financial writer. "I could probably have survived just fine in some Deep South hamlet, pretending to be the village eccentric. There are lots of unorthodox single women in the South — all you need to do is be fairly good-humored about it and take care to look completely asexual. In one way you'd have an easier time being gay in the South than up here. Southerners are vicious about gay men, of course, and they sense it out quickly. But homosexual women upset them so much they won't admit we exist. I'm not aggressively lesbian. I don't make a big thing of it. But I don't want to live in a place where deviation in a woman is so unthinkable that people won't own up to the possibility. Women like me find themselves declared nonexistent by local fiat."

*   *   *

Perhaps not one in a hundred of today's emigrés has ever heard of Sarah and Angelina Grimké, a pair of sisters from South Carolina who took their stand on the northern side of the Mason-Dixon line in the 1820s. They were probably not the first women to flee the Southland, but they were the first to leave any coherent record of their reasons. They were a splendid pair of early American radicals, a paradigm for many another rebellious spirit since, and anyone who doubts the inexorable continuity of the Southern experience has only to look at the Grimké sisters. What drove them out of their native state a hundred and fifty years ago were essentially the same forces that sent so many women northward in the 1960s and 1970s. Sarah and Angelina were at odds with their family and their milieu on the subject of race; but beyond that, they were unwilling and unable to assume their proper role as Southern ladies.

Sarah was born in 1792, Angelina, in 1805, the daughters of classic Charleston aristocrats of the sort who turn up in historical novels. Their father, John Grimké, of Huguenot descent, was a lawyer, judge, and rich planter, the holder of large numbers of slaves. Their mother, Mary, also from old money and old blood, was queen of the home in the grand manner. A couple of dozen servants were required to keep the Charleston town-house in order, and many more worked the rice plantation near Beaufort, where the family spent the winters. With the responsibilities of such a household, in addition to her life in Charleston society, Mary Grimké apparently had little time for her children — there were fourteen of them — but each of them had a nursemaid, and there was a supervisory mammy for the lot. By no means was the training of any small Grimké neglected — indeed, in a home so populous it must have been hard for a child to find a corner to be solitary in.

Sarah and Angelina both ought to have grown into highspirited if pious belles, sharpening their feminine wiles and practicing fine stitchery until at length they were suitably married, whereupon like dutiful barn swallows, they would have recommenced the cycle. Instead, Sarah grew up a lonely, odd little girl, full of unthinkable notions and ambitions. She was passionately religious with an excessive purism that must have been an irritation to her family, who were themselves undeviating Presbyterians. According to the recent biography of the sisters by Gerda Lerner, Sarah was a bright student who pleaded for permission to study Latin and then law, an ominous request that her father swiftly refused. She was twelve when Angelina was born — old enough to be dreaming of ball gowns and suitors if she had been a proper daughter. But instead she insisted upon standing godmother to her infant sister and then almost literally became her mother.

Together, as Angelina grew up, the two of them committed the ultimate apostasy for two young ladies of Charleston: they learned to hate slavery, and their hatred was not private and personal, compounded equally of hatred for the institution and for the Negroes (as, for example, Mary Chesnut's would be in the next generation), but philosophical and devastatingly well reasoned. As serious Christians, Sarah and Angelina dismissed the notion that Christianity could countenance slavery. Morever, they were the first American women to see — and say — that the enslavement of blacks entailed the enslavement of women and that without a class of compliant white females slavery would come to an end.

Though the Grimké family was as cultivated, as genteel, as any in Charleston, and Charleston was the very throne of old Southern culture, Sarah and Angelina had no trouble observing, right at home and in their neighbors' parlors, all the horrors of slavery. Years after leaving the South, Sarah told how a Charleston lady of her acquaintance, a churchgoing Christian, had dealt with a runaway slave woman. First, the lady had the slave whipped and one of her front teeth pulled out, as an identifying mark. Then she had her fitted with a heavy, three-pronged iron collar that prevented her from lying down except on her flayed back. "This slave," wrote Sarah, "who was the seamstress of the family, was continually in her mistress' presence, sitting in her chamber to sew or engaged in other housework with her lacerated and bleeding back, her mutilated mouth and heavy iron collar, without, so far as appeared, exciting any feelings of compassion."

As a schoolgirl, Angelina had fainted in the classroom when a slave boy had come in on some errand, his back so shredded that he could scarcely walk. She wrote of hurrying past the "workhouse," where slaves were sent to be beaten by professional "masters" and otherwise tortured (depending upon their owners' whims) and of hearing cries that she could not answer; she heard them, figuratively, the rest of her life. Most other people were unimpressed by such things. (Slaves and children had to be punished, according to the Bible.) And besides the studied brutality, there was all the rest of the inevitable misery.

When John Grimké died and his slaves were sold off, no one but the two sisters worried about the families that were broken up. And the Grimké men, like many others, casually crossed the color bar when they wanted black women. After Emancipation, when Sarah and Angelina were old and had lived for many years in rural New Jersey with Angelina's husband, the abolitionist Theodore Weld, they discovered that they had three black nephews, the children of one of their brothers. They welcomed the boys into the family and put them all through college.

Sarah had left Charleston in 1821, having converted to the Quaker religion, and settled down in Philadelphia, where she lived on the mercies of acquaintances she had made in the Society of Friends and on her income from a small inheritance. As Gerda Lerner observes, her family was scandalized by the spectacle of a single woman going off alone to a strange city. On the other hand, they may have been glad to be rid of her. In 1829 Angelina followed her sister to Philadelphia. Over the next few years, through the Quaker organization, the two sisters began working in the abolitionist cause. Among other works, Angelina produced an antislavery pamphlet called *Appeal to the Christian Women of the Southern States*, which made her so famous that the Charleston police promised they would arrest her on sight and deport her if she ever came home again.

But Angelina's ambitions lay northward at that point. She had trained herself to speak in public, and she intended to go on a lecture tour as an agent of the Female Anti-slavery Society. In 1838 she and Sarah set out; they went from church to town hall all over New England, and Angelina's long, impassioned orations on behalf of abolition attracted enormous audiences. On February 21, 1838, she even addressed the Massachusetts legislature. Here were two sheltered, aristocratic women from the heart of Charleston, stumping around New England like menfolks, joining up with dangerous radicals, and speaking out for abolition, of all things. If Sarah and Angelina had turned into cockroaches, it would have horrified their relatives in Charleston, and the general public, considerably less.

The horror of it, of course, was not merely their abolitionism but their determination to link that cause with feminism. In the 1830s scarcely anyone besides the Grimkés had even raised the subject of women's rights in this country. Not until 1848 would Elizabeth Cady Stanton call her celebrated convention in Seneca Falls, New York, and launch the women's suffrage movement. But here was Angelina, writing, "Women ought to feel a peculiar sympathy in the colored man's wrong, for, like him, she has been accused of mental inferiority, and denied the privileges of a liberal education." Sarah, perhaps the more dedicated feminist of the pair, was the author of a tract entitled *Letters on the Equality of the Sexes*. Its demands would sound familiar enough today — equal pay for equal work, the right to an education, full political equality, the acceptance of women into the clergy.

Sarah was not attacking the strictures on only Southern women. From the practical point of view, Northern women had the same legal rights as Southern ones, which was to say none. All the same, upper-class Southern women had an additional shackle, and she had acquired her aversion for the nineteenth-century notion of women's proper place just where the notion of womanhood had presumably reached its palmiest perfections, in the upper echelons of the Old South, where Arthurian chivalry had presumably been reinvented. What Sarah was courageous enough to say was that Southern women, in return for little or nothing, were collaborating in a collective criminal act that dehumanized women almost as much as it did slaves. No wonder Charleston was outraged.

Had Sarah not emigrated, how would her hometown have contained her? As it was, even in New England she and her

sister caused a scandal. When it came to radical abolitionism and unconventional female behavior, the press and the
clergy of New England were no more open-minded than
their brethren in the slave states. In sermons and newspaper articles they ridiculed the sisters as old maids, accused
them of lusting after black men, and thundered at them for
violating the laws of God. Even the most vociferous abolitionist of all, William Lloyd Garrison, was a little afraid of
them. He took a nervous view of the "woman question" and
the harm it might do the antislavery movement. Besides
being feminists, Sarah and Angelina were more radical on
abolition than Garrison. Vowing that they had seen too
much of slavery to be gradualists and that the deportation
of the freedmen would be a travesty of principle, they opposed all colonization schemes, such as Garrison's, for
sending the Negroes back to Africa. Even the dottiest left-
wingers thought the sisters were crazy. Like other emigrés
after them, Sarah and Angelina found out that if Charleston was no paradise, neither was Boston.

And yet the journey northward set them free. The South,
though it claims to be the cradle of rebellion, has never
tolerated nonconformism in its women. Charleston in this
epoch would surely have found a way to wall these rebels
off. Had she stayed at home, Sarah would either have gone
mad in time or turned into a rigidly pious maiden lady,
mortifying her flesh and doing good works, hanging on list-
lessly in some corner of her parents' house. Angelina, instead of making speeches in public and marrying an abolitionist, would no doubt have laid her crazy ideas aside,
married an acceptable gentleman like her father, swallowed
up her guilt as best she could, and been an exceptionally
kind mistress to her servants. Her diary — in which she
might timidly have expressed a few unorthodox opinions —
would now be carefully preserved in the air-conditioned
vaults of a university library, waiting for some Ph.D. can-
didate to unlock it.

When I left the South, I was impelled by none of the
saintly motives that drove Angelina and Sarah Grimké. At

that time I didn't know they existed, nor would I have cared. I went because, though a hundred and fifty years had passed since Sarah was refused permission to study Latin and law, there still was no place in the South for educated women except the schoolroom: no jobs and no men. Or so I thought. Besides that, I either had to cast my lot with those who said there was nothing wrong in the South except that "we" were being carpetbagged again, or I had to cease being a Southerner. Not, of course, that I had the slightest intention of going north and doing anything for racial justice. I just wanted to go someplace where I could feel good. I didn't know there were scores of others like me and unlike me. What I wanted I didn't know. But as I searched for it — money, independence, or maybe just a job — I meant once and for all to shed the ladylike ethic.

* * *

Sandra Cason is an emigré of another kind. Most of her colleagues knew her as Casey Hayden, a soft-spoken, idealistic young woman from east Texas who was a full-time worker in the civil rights movement in the early 1960s. For two years then she was married to Tom Hayden, who went on to become a kind of superstar radical of the decade and, as Jane Fonda's husband, is still a celebrity. Sandra Cason has been married and divorced another time since. She is forty now, tall and fair, with a modest manner but the self-possession of a veteran. When I talked with her in a restaurant in lower Manhattan, she was working nearby at the time as an editor on a weekly newspaper. She has since migrated to Boulder, Colorado.

Casey was born in Victoria, Texas, a country town on the southern perimeter. She left the South early in 1961, having graduated from the University of Texas, but her stay in the North was brief. After a few months at the University of Illinois, she went to Atlanta and then westward into Mississippi. She was one of the first field workers for the Student Non-violent Coordinating Committee, which from its headquarters in Atlanta sent its members out into the backwaters of Georgia, Alabama, and Mississippi. Their intention, simply stated, was to bring segregation down. They intended to work by peaceful means, and their ambitions were ultimately grandiose: SNCC's avowed purpose was to establish "a social order of justice, permeated by love." And in the beginning, many of the volunteers believed that they could do it.

This loosely knit clan of young radicals, many of them poor and black, willingly went out to picket and demonstrate in the streets and then just as willingly faced the fire hoses, the sheriffs' deputies, the beatings, the jails. Some of them may have been less than honest about their motivations; some, eventually corrupt. But they had courage. The most visible and vocal leadership was black and male. James Forman, Stokely Carmichael, and Julian Bond were the names most often in the newspapers, but at first most SNCC workers were white Southerners, predominantly white women like Sandra Cason. She was propelled into civil rights activism not by politics but by her religious convictions. She had come out of the plain Southern Protestant tradition that took the Bible literally in its teaching that God's children ought to love one another.

She grew up happily in Victoria, she says, the only child in a household of four adults — her mother and aunt, both divorced, and her two grandparents. Her grandfather was the county sheriff and a heavy drinker, a kind of functioning alcoholic. Casey's mother and aunt worked to support the family. The three women and the child took care not to mention grandfather's habits. They had an unacknowledged pact to protect themselves — and him — against the truth: "It was a very Southern thing to do. We just never admitted it." What changed Casey's life were her years at the University of Texas. Instead of becoming a sorority pledge, as she had once hoped to be, she joined the YWCA, which was one of the first organizations to rally to the integrationist cause. She also chose to live in the only integrated student house on campus, the Christian Faith and

Life Community. When the YWCA began to picket and stage sit-ins at segregated restaurants in Austin in 1960, Casey took part. By then her commitment was made:

"At the time I was not reacting consciously against any kind of Southern feminine mystique. I hardly knew there was such a thing. I realized, of course, that I was not acting the way a Southern girl was expected to act. I knew that most people thought I should not associate with blacks, particularly not black men. But I just thought they were wrong. Later it became clear to me that there was no longer a place for me in the South. After I left the movement in 1966, I thought of settling down in Atlanta, but I didn't know which side of town to live on. I would have been unwelcome in the black community, but I couldn't see myself as a white Southern liberal either. So I went to New York."

In the middle of the decade the coalition of blacks and whites in SNCC broke apart. Stokely Carmichael and his followers invented the concept of black power, which replaced brotherhood as an organizational goal. The coalition of men and women broke apart as well, for many women in the movement had grown angry about their own low status within the ranks. "The paperwork was always assigned to me," Casey remarks. In 1965 she and SNCC associate Mary King wrote and published what they called "a kind of memo." Entitled "Sex and Caste," it has its place in the history of the modern feminist movement. It is the earliest expression of the radical feminist tide that came directly out of the civil rights movement — much as Sarah and Angelina Grimké's feminist sentiments had grown out of their work for abolition.

"There seem to be many parallels that can be drawn between treatment of Negroes and treatment of women in our society," wrote Sandra Cason and Mary King. "Women . . . in the movement seem to be caught up in a common-law caste system that operates, sometimes subtly, forcing them to work around or outside hierarchical structures of power which may exclude them." The rhetoric has a bland, laborious, bureaucratic flavor. Stokely Carmichael's comment on the "kind of memo" was brief and blunt: "The only position for women in SNCC is prone."

Though Casey might have gone from the civil rights movement to the feminist one, she went instead into social work among the Northern ghetto poor and then into her second marriage, from which she has two children. Other women, none of them Southern, took the next step after "Sex and Caste" and made it the beginning of a new radicalism, perhaps the only piece of 1960s radicalism that lasted through the next decade. Casey is not opposed to the feminist movement, but she has kept her distance from it, as the Grimké sisters themselves kept their distance from the suffrage movement of the nineteenth century:

"I don't wish to speak critically of the feminist movement. I am not part of it and have no friends who are part of it just now. So my impressions of it come mostly from the press, which I know from experience distorts everything. But feminist thinking does not go deep enough. Mass American culture does not care about children and does not appreciate physical work. In our economy work is not valued for itself. It is something that is used to create money for the people who put up the goods. Women's work in the home, and what women do for children, is therefore seen as something not worthwhile. But the answer is not for everyone to work in offices but to reevaluate the worth of the work that is done in the home. I don't go for day-care centers. I know they are necessary sometimes, but as a way of nurturing, of creating human lives, I don't see it. I believe in a one-to-one relationship for children. I think the questions that have to be raised about our culture are much deeper than the ones the feminist movement has asked."

* * *

Some Southern emigrés have never left the South at all or even considered leaving it. (There are many ways of leaving besides on a bus or a plane.) The ultimate piece of nonconformism for a Southern woman is bookishness or any ostentatious devotion to learning. It is even more likely to isolate her from her class than are radical commitments or professional ambitions. In his memoir *Southern Legacy* the late Hodding Carter, a distinguished newspaper editor and Mississippi liberal, set down the wicked truth: "An uncanny sixth sense — or perhaps just simple observation — has made the Southern woman aware that the otherwise heroic Southern male is abjectly afraid of erudite females. Beauty unsupported we can understand and appreciate. Beauty and an outward show of brains — from all such combinations we shy away." Carter was too polite to carry the proposition to its third step, which is that braininess unsupported by beauty does more than terrify the average Southern male. It strikes him as disgusting and unnatural.

Despite all this, or possibly because of it, the South is not without its cadre of learned women. As a group they are not showy; those I have known live in semidetachment from Southern life. They are often single; they often form the core of the faculty at women's colleges, where they try to focus the often-distracted minds of their young students upon the intricacies of western civilization. In the South as elsewhere up to now, the preponderance of doctorates is awarded to men, and hence so are most professorships. But at some Southern women's colleges, particularly in the liberal arts fields, women teachers have traditionally outnumbered the men. Erudition may be a serious flaw in a female, but in academe there are ways of accommodating it, even nurturing it as a useful countercultural trend.

According to Margaret Pepperdene, the present Chairman of the English Department at Agnes Scott College in Decatur, Georgia, the mere presence of scholarly women at the head of a classroom can be helpful in building a student's self-esteem. "For the first time in their lives, our students see women in positions of intellectual authority. They begin to believe that women can compete with men academically. They gain a sense of self. I had a student some years ago who went to Harvard to get her doctorate. The very first woman professor had only just been appointed in the English department, and the students were amazed. They went off to hear the 'lady professor' lecture — out of pure curiosity." Dr. Pepperdene is a good-looking, outspoken woman in her late fifties, with a combination of "beauty and an outward show of brains," potent enough to stun any otherwise heroic Southern male.

In a culture that only reluctantly excuses the anomaly of erudition in a female, the love of learning sometimes becomes a calling, rather than a profession. "I am a born-again humanist," Dr. Pepperdene says, "and the happiest days of my career, I think, were my first years here at the college. I had no administrative responsibilities, so I could simply bury myself in English literature, reading poetry for weeks, uninterrupted, ten hours a day if I chose, just for the pleasure of it. No one in those days called it research. I believe in the liberal arts; I could go around the country preaching them. Most of our students marry and do not immediately put their education to any professional use. And yet I believe that what they learn here provides them with an inner self-respect, something to keep them sane."

But there are risks in the life of the inner emigré. Just as the belle may begin as a conniver and end up believing that she really is helpless and dumb, the scholar isolated within the walls may turn into a pedant. Few women go to the extremes of a Southern fugitive I know — whom I shall call Clara Jo Miles — who taught at a Virginia women's college. She was the chairman of the history department. A strict constructionist in syntactical matters, as in all else, she would have died rather than call herself a chairwoman, let alone a chairperson. She loathed all forms of modernity and almost all men and certainly all Jews and blacks. As an officer in her national professional society, she was often obliged to travel. She loathed that, too. When in New York, she made a point of staying at the Barbizon Hotel for women, not having willingly slept under the same roof with a man since the death of her father. She always hired a limousine, no matter what the cost, in order to avoid dealing with cab drivers. She would probably have worn a gas mask if she could have found one. Once in New Orleans, as she told it with/a touch of malicious pride, she had contracted food poisoning from eating an improperly washed lettuce leaf and had had to be rushed unconscious to the hospital.

As department head she often received letters from newly minted Ph.D.'s in search of work. Her secretary told me that males and all applicants with suspicious combinations of consonants in their surnames went immediately into the wastebasket. When Dr. Miles had been appointed chairman, the history faculty had consisted of six women and one old man who had finally died after keeping Dr. Miles in an irritating state of expectation for five years. She wasn't about to pollute the atmosphere again. ("They can always find positions up north.")

She expected her best students to emulate her in this restrictive form of misanthropy. After the manner of the cruel ballet impresario in *The Red Shoes*, she looked upon love and marriage as second-rate pastimes designed for dimwits. Any students suspected of being affianced were either crossed off the list of potential star scholars, or told to write twenty-page papers on the legal rights of women in the eighteenth-century Shropshire.

Her own scholarly accomplishments consisted of two monumentally learned books on the Wars of the Roses. Substantively inconsequential, these works were models of their genre. So perfectly differentiated were the *op.cit.'s* from the *loc.cit.'s*, the *ibid.'s* from the *viz.'s* and the *sic's*, so jammed were they with evidence from previously unexamined papers in the private libraries of English peers, that they had become minor classics. Had any normal, genial Southern male ever looked inside one of these works struck off by a woman's pen, he would have thought them ludicrous or stupefying. They were Dr. Miles's iron fist in the face of contemporary mindlessness, her chain fence set up against pop culture, her answer to the vulgarians who wrote history for buffs.

On top of it all she was a perfect lady, delicate and teeny

tiny. No diminutive could be too extreme for her. Her coats would have fit any healthy eleven-year-old. At night she did her gray hair up in minute spit-curls which showed the track of the bobby pins by day. Her transparent hands were those of a late Victorian consumptive: too weak, one might have imagined, to lift a quill from an inkwell. (She did, in fact, wield her Schaefer in an extraordinary way, between her index and middle fingers, as if she lacked a thumb.) She had only two attributes of any size: a pair of vast blue eyes, cold and innocent. Alexander Pope, "the wicked wasp of Twickenham," as his enemies called him and the only poet Dr. Miles ever quoted, must have had just such eyes. Dressed in her gabardine suite with a lacy bow at the throat of her blouse, seated on a monstrous cushion so she could see over the wheel of her Packard, Dr. Miles might have been just another little grandmotherly figure on her way to some-body's garden tea. But she was an impostor, for she had coolly rejected the most basic law of the ladylike code which says that women are born to serve and manage men (per-haps even to love them), and that female brains, if any, are to be kept from view. And so, unwilling or too proud to leave her native place, she had walled herself up so tightly that a mere lettuce leaf from the outside world was enough to render her insensible.

Clara Jo Miles was definitely not the sort of female intel-lectual usually called a bluestocking. That is a distinctively Northern epithet with no Southern equivalent in language or in life. Willie Morris, as an immigrant to Manhattan, described how he was set upon by one of these at a literary cocktail party — "a longlegged Eastern bluestocking with Gauloise smoke curling out of her ample nostrils blamed me for the institution of slavery, the Compromise of 1877, the Jim Crow laws, and the riots in Watts, and ended up, after two more drinks, identifying me as 'poor white trash.'" No wonder he was startled. No Southern woman ever at-tacks a man with abstractions. I am probably a closet bluestocking myself, but I had been in the North ten years before I was able to challenge a man on ideological grounds, and when I managed to express a contrary opinion, I betrayed a craven willingness to retreat and hedged every phrase with "I think," and "you know," and "I *mean*," and "things like that." (I even had that Southern female mannerism of giggling at the end of a sentence — just to show I retained my amateur status when it came to having opinions about Big Topics.

In the same essay which expresses his insights on female intellectuality and the easily affrighted Southern male, Hodding Carter went on to provide an instructive tableau of the cultivated Southern woman in action. His wife Betty, whom he describes as the "researcher, editor, and consultant for everything I write," was herself a writer, and he relates with some pride that she had spent the winter months writing a paper about T. S. Eliot, largely for her own pleasure. Then, in the spring, Harvard had summoned Carter to Cambridge to receive an honorary degree. It was 1947, and it happened that he shared the podium with T. S. Eliot. At the reception that followed, however, Mrs. Carter did not display any unseemly independence or even let on that she had ever heard of the poet. "She was just the little Southern helpmeet, the wife so proud of her husband, every minute." Women, he concludes, were meant to be charming, not brainy, though he has to admit that it is often the women who "provide our only link with the great outside world of arts and letters." It seems that no matter how intelligent they are, they have to know their place. They have to stay in line. As Carter put it, "If the ultimate horror should descend upon us all, there will surely be heard at its end, somewhere in the radioactive wilderness of the survivors, a voice saying with unmistakable inflection and unchanging purpose: 'Honey, I've found some nice bricks for a chimney, but it'll take a strong man like you to stack them up, 'cause I'm just so helpless.' "

Betty Carter, as her husband describes her, was the positive atom that matched Dr. Miles's negative. In no sense was she an emigré, at least as she exists in *Southern Legacy*. She must have been the archetype of the bright, adaptive Southern woman who is able to play by the rules, the woman that I briefly imagined I could be. But not everybody can be so smooth. For those afflicted with incurable spiritual and intellectual gawkiness, emigration *in situ* is one solution — to become humanist hermits singing in the wilderness like Margaret Pepperdene or, at the other extreme, stylites perched balefully atop a desert column like Clara Jo Miles.

*   *   *

What lay in waiting for me at the other end of that plane ticket was a number of surprises. In the late 1950s, Southerners were still an oddity in New York, or at least white ones were. Even at large gatherings, I would be the only person with a Southern accent, and I got used to hearing people exclaim, "My God, I never met anybody from Arkansas before in my life." It was rather like being a Hottentot, but pleasantly so. At first I liked being the token Arkie. Then I discovered that all New Yorkers automatically assumed that all Southerners were lynch-mob veterans. Their hostility was usually fairly restrained, but I did have to recite my little loyalty oath: no, I had never been to a cross burning, and yes, my sentiments toward black people were entirely correct.

For a while I truly believed that theirs and mine were correct. My doubts began to take shape one day as I stood in a gallery of the Metropolitan Museum of Art surrounded by a group of well-dressed people who were eager to know what Harlem looked like and had come to an exhibition of photographs to find out. We all stood there in semidarkness as the slide projector flashed scene after scene from 125th Street, forty blocks north of the Museum. We were like Methodists at missionary circle, gawking at pictures from farthest Cathay.

At the time I was working at a publishing house where everybody was passionate about civil rights. We all sent donations to Martin Luther King and Stokely Carmichael, yet there was not one black face among us. Many of us belonged to a group that did, in fact, set foot in Harlem once a week to take part in tutoring high school students. But the gap between the races in New York City was a canyon of ice. In Alabama, people were engaging in hand-to-hand combat, which at least was newsworthy. I felt a little foolish sometimes, sitting opposite a pair of incredulous black teen-agers and explaining (in my redneck accent) how to conjugate irregular French verbs.

By then I had also wised up to the fact that to be female as well as Southern was construed as evidence of slow wits. New Yorkers assumed you were stupid, the way Californians had assumed you were diseased. I systematically re-formed my speech, patterning my vowels after the typical Vassar graduate's, or as near as I could get, vainly hoping no one would find me out. Anything I had to do seemed worth it, such was my relief at finding asylum and being allowed to live in a milieu where being both unmarried and educated were not crippling disqualifications for a woman.

As escapes go, mine was ambivalent and scarcely final. I soon discovered that the mystique that drove me out — the ideal of the Southern lady — was not peculiar to the South at all, simply more flamboyantly expressed there. And in any case, it was a sort of phony overlay to begin with —the real feminine mystique of the South lay with those strong women, those drowned women of the farm and the frontier. As for racism, the Northerner brand is in some ways even less palatable than the Southern. "It isn't that we would dislike having black children in our schools," a suburban P.T.A. member remarked to me recently. "It's just that black families can't afford to buy property in this area." Are the ghettos of New York any different from what used to be called "nigger towns" of the South — except for being dirtier, more dangerous, and even more utterly walled off from the white world?

And so I have been drawn back, for brief spaces, to my homeplace, and unlike the truly displaced, I have had the chance to hang on to my cultural identity, picky about it though I have been, and to watch the fortunes of my native place fall and rise again, as they have done in the past years. From afar I watched the South remake itself (without any aid from me) nearer to my childhood image of it: a benevolent place where the outward and sometimes even the inward forms of courtesy are scrupulously observed, where people remember your grandpa with respect even though he was a chicken farmer, where there was enough decency left, after the violence ran itself out, to rebuild the Southern school system. I have had the joy of keeping in touch, of going back to the family reunions, the weddings, the funerals (which have their peculiar joy too), of showing my children where I came from and offering them the chance to love what I love. Not many refugees have such luck.

Lately I go home in panic, for fear the South is gone. According to the news magazines, the solid block of eccentricity that lives within the boundaries of the old Confederate states has been gerrymandered into a rich, bland, hateful thing called the Sunbelt, which runs from Miami Beach to Arizona and, if my painful recollection is correct, even includes Colorado and New Mexico. But when I go home, it always calms me to see that Southern cities, however slick and new, don't quite seem citified.

While the South is not as slow and introverted and landlocked as it once was, it has not vanished. The plantation South has all but disappeared, and all traces of the frontier South will soon be gone — the dirt road leading to a house with a wood stove and an oak table piled high with cornbread and fried okra, or whatever reality and symbol one grasps at. Ten years from now, perhaps they will give up opening the old churchhouses on Decoration Day. They may stop weeding the graves and decorating the headstones with plastic roses or bothering to remember the middle names of a second cousin's five children. The frontier will nevertheless survive in the attitudes a few of us inherited from it. One of those attitudes — to me a beatitude — is the conviction that the past matters, that history weighs on us and refuses to be forgotten by us, and that the worst poverty women — or men — can suffer is to be bereft of their past.